To Jeff
May great Karma
be with
you...

CUSTOMER KARMA

Why Stop at a One-Night Stand, When You Can Have a Lifetime Relationship with Your Customers?

Arjun Sen

CUSTOMER KARMA
WHY STOP AT A ONE-NIGHT STAND, WHEN YOU CAN HAVE A LIFETIME RELATIONSHIP WITH YOUR CUSTOMERS?

Copyright © 2016 Arjun Sen.

All rights reserved. No part of this book may be used or reproduced by any means, graphic, electronic, or mechanical, including photocopying, recording, taping or by any information storage retrieval system without the written permission of the author except in the case of brief quotations embodied in critical articles and reviews.

iUniverse books may be ordered through booksellers or by contacting:

iUniverse
1663 Liberty Drive
Bloomington, IN 47403
www.iuniverse.com
1-800-Authors (1-800-288-4677)

Because of the dynamic nature of the Internet, any web addresses or links contained in this book may have changed since publication and may no longer be valid. The views expressed in this work are solely those of the author and do not necessarily reflect the views of the publisher, and the publisher hereby disclaims any responsibility for them.

Any people depicted in stock imagery provided by Thinkstock are models,
and such images are being used for illustrative purposes only.
Certain stock imagery © Thinkstock.

ISBN: 978-1-5320-0522-0 (sc)
ISBN: 978-1-5320-0524-4 (hc)
ISBN: 978-1-5320-0523-7 (e)

Library of Congress Control Number: 2016913202

Print information available on the last page.

iUniverse rev. date: 09/23/2016

This book is dedicated to
Trey Hall,
my best friend.

Trey was a born gentleman who was always there for his friends.
His brilliant marketing mind was defined
by his simple yet breakthrough thinking.
In the book, anytime I wrote about authenticity
and integrity, all I had to do was describe him.
I wish he had not left us before the book was finished.

Contents

Acknowledgments ix
The Purpose of the Book xi

Lessons on Good Karma 1
Karma Lessons from My Grandma 3
Karma in the Business World 8
Seeing the Big Picture First:
The Seven Blind Men and the Elephant 11
Understanding the Customer:
Are You a Butterfly or a Terminator Today? 15

Understanding Relationships 21
Humanizing Customer Relationships 23
A Journey Must Start with Self-Discovery 27
Start Strong 31
Making It Easy to Explore 36
Seeking Confirmation 39
The Grand Finale: Decision Time 44
What's Your Hurry, Cowboy? Savor the Moment 49

Good Karma in Communication 55
Don't Start as a Fire Hydrant 57
Random Taglines 60
Speak a Common Language 63
Bread-Crumbing Communication 67
The Science of Communication 70

Karma of Giving 75
When a Grandma Called Me Stupid 77
A Free Bra on My Birthday 82

No More Warm Nuts for Me 89
  Texting "XOXO" in the Middle of the Night 94
  My Pleasure? Really? 97

Start with Authenticity 101
  No Room for Trick Play 103
  Can't Believe You Made Me Feel Stupid 109
  Surprises from Friends and Family 112
  Strategizing Not to Get Caught 116
  A Warm Heart Always Gets Noticed 120
  True Integrity 123
  Making Fun of Others 126

Good Karma Is Not for Sale 131
  Loyalty Cannot Be Programmed 133
  Outsourcing Love 136
  Discounting Love 141
  Affection Disclaimers 145
  Showing Love with Just a Hot Towel 149

Be Focused and Add a Personal Touch 153
  Curly's One Thing 155
  Will Never Hit a 5-Iron Hybrid from a Fairway Bunker (Again) 159
  One of One and Not One of Many 161
  Surviving Challenges 165

The Journey to Better Karma 171
  Getting to Ever After 173
  Celebrating Your Top Customer 176
  Daring to Be Different 181
  Seeking Inspiration 187
  Disruption to Win Big 191
  Final Words 196

Endnotes 201

Acknowledgments

Inspiration Sources

Maiji,
my grandma, for being the Yoda in my life

Raka Sen
for her constant cheer and encouragement

Made This Book a Reality

Clint McCaskill
for making every aspect of the book better
and making sure I did not give up

Chitra Sen
for her support and being the number-one fan of the book

Clay Dover
for being a friend and believer

Contribution to the Book

• Ishan Benegal • Cody Roper • Alexandria Schultz • Mitch Sonderfan

My Gurus

• Scott Beck • Ken Calwell • Lane Cardwell • Tom Cole
• Warren Ellish • Reggie Fils-Aime • Blaine Hurst • John Lauck
• Jeff Lawson • Dan Paxton • John Schnatter • Marj Wilson
for passing on their experiential knowledge to me

The Purpose of the Book

Memo

To:	You
From:	Arjun Sen
Subject:	Why You Should Read This Book
Date:	February 5, 2016

Dear reader,

I wanted to put in front of you a few reasons you should read this book.

What Corporate Marketing and Operations Experience Taught Me

My corporate experience was the perfect place to learn about the importance of the total experience, as every experience is custom created for each guest. It also taught me that long-term success is all about transactions, or traffic. The number of transactions is the one number that is real. Even for a single store operator, success is defined by how many times he opens the cash register and how much money he puts in every time. If he is opening the cash register fewer times every day, he should be worried.[1]

My Corporate Background

After earning my undergraduate degree in aeronautical engineering from the Indian Institute of Technology in Kharagpur, India, and my MBA from Brigham Young University, I started my corporate career at Pizza Hut. Next, I worked with Boston Market, assisting the brand's evolution from Boston Chicken to Boston Market, and I was one of the founding members of Einstein Bros., instrumental in determining the guest experience for the brand.

In my last corporate job, as vice president of marketing and operation services for Papa John's International, I designed and implemented a guest-experience-focused online ordering system, the first system of its kind. Since the system's implementation, the pizza chain's revenue from online ordering has increased by more than 50 percent every year, and the company recently completed more than $1 billion in transactions. I was also part of the team that worked on the *Pizza Hut v. Papa John's* lawsuit, which has become a benchmark for one of the most successful comparative advertising campaigns.

My corporate experience can be best summarized by a quote from Blaine Hurst, ex-president of Papa John's, who called me "the go-to guy who makes things happen."

My Consulting Experience

Since 2001, I have been the president and CEO of ZenMango, a marketing consulting firm working with a variety of companies that include restaurants, retail brands, service brands, nonprofits and charities, academic institutions, top golf professionals, and other guest-experience-driven industries. In the book, I have included the commonality from all of my learning, and that is the essence of using customer karma to build a long-term relationship with customers.

Written in a Corporate Language You Can Relate To

In my office, I am surrounded by books with titles like *The New Way to ...*, *Five Steps to ...*, *Best Practices in ...*, and so on. I always felt two distinct high moments with every business book.

- The first one was when I bought the book. I felt a promise of a better future—the same way I felt when I got a new exercise machine.
- My second high came when I read the book and collected some great insights and learning. Often, I even made a cheat sheet of my takeaways from the book.

The business concepts in almost every business book I have read are brilliant, but when I was in the corporate trenches, facing deadlines and struggling with limited resources, business books never provided me with the solutions to my problems. Instead, I always reached out to friends who had gone through similar situations. I wrote the book in that spirit, to be your corporate buddy.

Lessons on Karma from My Grandma

When I grew up in India, I was fortunate to have my grandma as part of my everyday life. She was there for me, to be my cheerleader and my compass in life and to reflect on circumstances when things did not go well. She taught me the concept of karma, which empowers one to impact what one gets out of business relationships.

The Book's Promise

My vision for the book has been fun, no-nonsense experience sharing. It will not give you one road map for all situations; instead, it is sure to trigger thoughts on what you can do differently.

I thank you for your interest.

Enjoy the book!

Lessons on Good Karma

When I was working with a top sports personality, he asked me to stay focused on the present. He explained to me that focusing on the present helps you maximize the present. Later on, when one looks back, one can only celebrate and appreciate past success or learn from mistakes made.

This advice has been helpful to me, as I am grateful for every lesson I have learned in life. If I consider each lesson a valuable pearl, today, when I look back at them all together, I see them as a pearl necklace, together much more valuable to me than each individual pearl. All the combined learning has helped me understand what the path to good karma is and how a business can have good customer karma.

As I share my experiences, it is important for you to note that you must identify what karma is and isn't to you. That is essential to tapping into the power of karma in your life. Nearly everyone has heard the word *karma*. My grandma introduced me to the

word *karma* and the concepts connected with it. She illustrated the meaning of the word to me through simple examples. Let me share with you some of the lessons from my grandma, as her words have been my cornerstone of the concept of karma. Once we are on the same page about the concept of karma, I want to check to see if the concept works in the business world. I have learned that the following concepts set up the framework of karma in the business world.

- **Seeing the Big Picture First:** Seeing the big picture helps one put things in perspective. When one does that, it is easier to put the customer first.
- **Understanding People's Mind-Sets:** All people are not the same, and one person does not act the same way all the time. Understanding how customers react in different situations is essential before one decides how to treat them.

Karma Lessons from My Grandma

When I grew up in India, I was fortunate to have my grandma as part of my everyday life. She was there for me, to be my cheerleader and my compass in life and to reflect on circumstances when things did not go well. Reflecting on the past with her was one of the most critical elements of my growing up. She never told me the answer but always guided me to get there. I recall a series of experiences that helped me refine what karma was. We all have experiences, and perhaps these experiences can help you find similar concepts in your own life. Defining the concept of karma is essential to understanding it, and my grandmother was instrumental in helping me do so.

Ninety-Nine Percent in Third-Grade Math Was Not Enough

One of the earliest situations I can think of was a math test in third grade. I was proud of my math abilities and was confident that I'd aced the midterm. When the results came in, my score was a 99 out of 100. The teacher explained to me that she'd deducted one point for lack of neatness. I was heartbroken. I came home and started crying, blaming the teacher for being cruel and robbing me of my well-deserved perfect score.

My grandma listened to me and then said, "You have the graded paper with you, don't you? This evening, I want you to grade that paper on your own—but only from a neatness point of view. Let me know what you feel, but remember—you are only looking at the neatness and nothing else."

That evening, I went over the paper. I started with confidence that there would be no reason whatsoever in the paper for her to have given me anything less than a perfect score. As I went through the paper, I realized there were quite a few instances in which I had erased my work clumsily and written over the unclearly erased text. In one instance, I could even argue that for a specific problem, it was not clear what my final answer was. The teacher had been kind enough to give me the benefit of the doubt. Later that evening, when I sat with my grandma, she asked me, "Were you perfect in the neatness area? Was your lack of neatness an issue in showcasing your work or the final answer in any question?" I had to admit that I had been sloppy and had not taken neatness seriously. In fact, I had been lucky to get the full points on a problem where the teacher could have deducted more points. That day, my grandma taught me two important lessons in life.

1. Anytime I got results that were not favorable, I should focus first on what I had done and then on what I could have done differently. Focusing on others or blaming others was convenient, but that never would help me get better.
2. Results would always be a function of my effort and actions. I needed to be perfect first before I could expect perfect results.

Regretting Not Making the School Quiz Team

Another time, I was trying to be on the school quiz team. I went to the tryouts and did not make it. I was disappointed. This time, my grandma was kind and gentle. She started by saying, "Don't worry. Next time, you will do better." Then she went on to say, "Did you have a clear idea about how to prepare for the quiz selections? If you had a clear idea, then did you prepare as much as you would have liked to?" As I thought about her questions, I realized the answer to both was no. I had had some idea about the scope of the quiz and studied a little, but I'd been sure that what I knew was enough to get me through. The more I thought, the more I realized that my lack of knowledge of the scope of the quiz and my lack of preparation had not aligned well with my false confidence of succeeding. To succeed, I should have had more clarity of what was required of me and then put in my best efforts. Only then could I have expected to have a real chance of succeeding.

Sanskrit Teacher Did Not Like Me

Then there was the time I told my grandma that my Sanskrit language teacher did not like me. This time, my grandma thought my reaction was funny. I was not amused by the fact that she thought my predicament was funny. I told her that the teacher not liking me was seriously costing me in class, as he would never call on me. As she learned that it was important for me to get the teacher to like me, she asked me, "Does the teacher even know your name? Do you know what the teacher likes? What effort, other than waiting to be called on in class, have you made for the teacher to like you?" As I listened to her, it was clear to me that my complaining to my grandma about my teacher would not change the situation. I needed to proactively take steps to change things, as that was in my control.

Karma Defined Applying for My Engineering Entrance Exam

As I grew older, my grandma helped me connect the dots in each of these learning moments. One evening, when we were sitting on the balcony, I told her that after finishing high school, I wanted to be an engineer. I wanted to graduate from India's top engineering college, one of the six Indian Institutes of Technology. She smiled at me and said, "It is all about your karma." I was confused, as I thought karma meant fate. Was my grandma telling me that everything was dependent on fate, which meant I did not have to do anything other than wait for fate to reveal itself? Was there nothing I could do to ensure I got into the IITs? My grandma went on to explain, "Karma comes from the Sanskrit word *karman*, which means 'action' or 'doing.' I am referring to what you can do in any situation. You must have a clear idea of what is required to get into the IITs and then go do your best. Then you can tell yourself that you have done your best, meaning you did the right karma. Only then will you have the best chance of getting in." I was starting to see what she was saying. Grandma went on to say, "There are no shortcuts to success. Success is hardly ever bestowed on those who do not work hard or do good karma. Do good karma, and you will be rewarded with good karma."

ning, I could confidently say that I got it. I started understanding the lessons of karma. I studied hard, did my karma, and was rewarded with an admission to the IITs. I graduated from IIT Kharagpur with a degree in aerospace engineering. After that, I came to the United States, earned my MBA, and got into the corporate world in the field of consumer marketing. In my years of working with some of the top consumer brands in the fields of restaurants, retail, service, and consumer goods, I learned that the concept of karma was the be-all and end-all definer of success. To me, the concept of karma was a blend of Newton's third law of physics, which states, "For every action, there is an equal and opposite reaction," and the golden rule, which states, "One should treat others as one would like others to treat oneself." In my career, the more clarity I got about karma and its effects, the more I could successfully understand consumer behavior and the corporate world. A defining moment came to me when I was talking to the CEO of a company and asked him, "How do people get promoted in the corporate world?"

He explained to me in simple terms, "You get promoted when the right person comes at the right time and witnesses you doing the right thing. You cannot influence who the right person is, nor can you influence when he will come to witness you. But you can inspire yourself to do the right thing every day every moment so that when the right person comes, he will for sure witness you doing the right thing."

Wow, I thought. I felt the CEO had simply stated in different words what my grandma had said as I was growing up: "Arjun, just keep doing good karma. Then you will be rewarded with good karma in return."

As I have reflected on my grandma's words over the years, I have distilled this knowledge into three clear steps of doing good karma.

1. To determine karma in a situation, start by understanding what good karma is. Seeing the big picture puts things into perspective and impacts the decisions you will make. Then pause. Pausing and

having this clarity is important, just as it is important for you to clearly know where you are going before you start your journey.
2. Next, commit to putting your best effort toward doing good karma. My grandma reinforced this idea by telling me over and over that there are no shortcuts to success. Good karma happens only when you put forth your best effort.
3. Finally, if the results do not come out as desired, reflect back on the first two steps above. Did you clearly identify what was good karma in this situation? Did you do your best? You can only focus on what you could have done differently, and thinking of other factors will take away the opportunity to self-reflect and get better.

These lessons translated well in the business world, where focusing on the big picture is essential to determining how well you can retain customers.

Karma in the Business World

A closer look at the concept of karma shows that causality is a big part of it. Over the years, I have learned that my grandma's advice about karma is relevant in the corporate world too. As I share the impact of karma in the business world, you will see how causality plays a strong role in defining karma in this world.

The journey to write the book came from my search for the meaning of life in the business world. I started with the realization that life in this world was more than simply sales growth or increased profits. It was more than a new product launch that raised the stock price. Over time, I realized the meaning of life in this world was all about building a lifetime relationship with your customers. If your business has a lifelong relationship with its customers, then sales are guaranteed to grow.

Valuation of Coffee Shop Karma

Imagine you are running a coffee shop. A customer comes to you three times a week, and every time, he spends approximately $8. You put your heart into building a relationship with the customer. Then the following happens.

- In one week, the customer spends $24 with you.
- In a month, he spends approximately $100.
- In a year, he spends approximately $1,200.
- In five years, he spends approximately $6,000.

Now that you see the value of the customer to be $6,000 every five years, you are surely going to look at him differently. You will have no problem putting in extra effort to build a relationship with this customer. Now add the concept of causality. Giving him great customer service comes first. Only if you provide great service will he spend $6,000 with you for five years. It does not work the other way. You cannot expect the customer to come to you one day and say, "If I buy $6,000 worth of food and beverages from you over the next five years, will you please give me great customer service?"

This causality of offering great service to the customer and getting rewarded in the long term is exactly what my grandma taught me about karma. Think of the coffee shop example. In the example, doing good karma for the customer involves being friendly to him and going above and beyond to make him happy every day, and that can result in $6,000 revenue over a five-year period. Now, if that is not good karma for the coffee shop, I do not know what is. Just know that my grandma was never wrong, as good customer karma defines any brand's future success.

Customer Complaints Are Opportunities

Here are some other examples of simple gestures that are good investments in customer karma.

- It is raining hard, and the customer asks the retail store clerk if he can borrow an umbrella. The store clerk's first reaction might be worry that the customer will not bring the umbrella back. However, helping the customer by lending him an umbrella might be a great way to connect with the customer and plant the seed for a potential long-term relationship.
- A customer calls the customer service line of a digital entertainment company, complaining that the new video game he has just ordered does not work. The customer service representative (CSR) might be tempted to verify that the game is actually not working before he plans to send out a replacement. If the CSR pauses for a moment, he will realize that the customer has already proven his desire to own the game by buying it and is now calling because he cannot play the game. If the CSR finds a way to kill the downtime by getting

the customer a link to a download so that he can start playing the game without any further delay, that will be good karma directed toward the customer. That is bound to strengthen the relationship between the customer and the brand and might earn the brand off-the-charts word of mouth. The customer might go on social media and write, "Can you believe what they did? I called, and within minutes, they sent me a link. As I was downloading the link, they got all the information from me, but I was up and playing within fifteen minutes of calling them. Impressive."

Examples like these are opportunities that can be found in any business nearly every day. All a brand needs to do is seize these opportunities and do good customer karma consistently and spontaneously. The results will speak for themselves.

Seeing the Big Picture First: The Seven Blind Men and the Elephant

As I start emphasizing the importance of seeing the whole picture instead of just seeing the parts, I think of a story my grandma told me from ancient India. This was one of my favorite stories growing up, and my grandma would act out different parts of the narrative during her storytelling. In the fascinating story of "The Seven Blind Men and the Elephant," the king brought an elephant to seven blind men and asked them to guess what it was. Each man walked around the elephant, touched it, and then came up with his conclusion based completely on his personal experience. The first man felt the tail and thought the object was a rope. The next man stepped up and touched the leg, and he believed it was a pillar. Another man touched the tip of the tail and thought it was a brush. The man who touched the elephant's ear thought the object was a winnowing basket. The other three men also had different conclusions based only on their experiences.

What I find fascinating is that each blind man truly did his diligent exploration and came up with a conclusion that could be entirely justified based on the experience he had. But not once did any of them think that he could be partially right or that there was a bigger truth than his personal experience. If the men had paused and seen the elephant from a different angle or collaborated to see the whole picture, they might have been able to figure out that the brush, basket, pillar, and rope were parts of an elephant. The incomplete story prevented them from maximizing the opportunity and being aware of the threat in front of them. This story showcases how focusing on one piece of the puzzle can often be misleading.

Designing the World's Largest Aircraft

I am sure there are moments in life when all of us act as one of the blind men in the "The Seven Blind Men and the Elephant." My moment came when I was studying aerospace engineering at the Indian Institute of Technology in Kharagpur. In my final year of aerospace engineering school, I was working on a cross-functional project that required me to find a solution for transporting a payload from point A to point B. I collaborated with different faculty members on aerodynamics, the aircraft structure, the propulsion, and other critical areas. I made decent progress in each functional area, but when I put all the parts together, I realized that I had designed an absurdly long airplane. What followed were frantic meetings with different faculty members to discuss the areas of the project. In the initial phase of the discussions, the faculty members all focused primarily on their areas, wanting to make sure there was nothing wrong in their parts of the process. In this phase, I experienced the brilliance of each faculty member, but their focus on only their individual areas of specialization felt comparable to the seven blind men, with all of them justifying why their observations that the elephant was a rope or a brush were right. The difference between the blind men and my faculty members was that the faculty did not stubbornly stay stuck in their points of view. After they went in depth in their own functional areas, they started collaborating and broadening their visions of the overall bigger picture. They started showing how connected their fields of expertise were.

The initial design of the absurdly long aircraft made me learn a lot about the different functional areas of aeronautical engineering, but what was a bigger education to me personally was learning that individual parts could never be greater than the whole. I realized that a lot of us focus on parts, as it is easier to focus on parts than to try to look at the whole picture. Connecting to an imaginary big picture takes a leap of faith, and that throws a lot of us outside our comfort zones.

As I evolved in the corporate world, I noticed that being aware of the entire picture was essential for me to solve a problem successfully. Being aware of only the parts and starting to fix the problem without looking picture might result in a quicker solution, but it might not ne the best solution. Let me illustrate this with an example.

How Boston Chicken Became Boston Market

In 1995, when I was working at Boston Chicken, the company decided to change their business focus and become Boston Market. It was not just a name change, as the company was evolving from being just a restaurant to a distribution point for home meals. The CEO, Scott Beck, being a visionary, felt that success of the transition would directly depend on how well each individual team member connected to the change. To assist the team, he came up with a unique plan. Here are some of the highlights of the plan.

- Each team member had to identify the critical three areas he or she was working on and have a clear idea of how they connected to the business goals.
- Each team member then had a conversation with his or her direct supervisor to make sure that their views on the critical three areas aligned and discuss how they connected to the big picture.
- Next, each team member posted the critical three areas in his or her cubicle or office.
- All team members were encouraged to walk around and read other team members' critical three areas and start conversations on them.

This process took a month to implement, but once implemented, it did three things:

1. It gave every team member a clear idea of the three things he or she should be working on.
2. It provided a clearer idea of the big picture of the company and how the employees' tasks connected to that.
3. It gave each team member a clearer idea of what others were working on, creating an opportunity for better synergy and teamwork.

This idea from Scott Beck was instrumental in assisting the organization through the change successfully. As you look at this example, you should realize that seeing the big picture pays not only during big changes but also in the running of the everyday business.

Understanding the Customer: Are You a Butterfly or a Terminator Today?

I want to explore how people react in everyday life. There are times when our interactions in the business world become too formal or forced. In the corporate world, we write contracts in ways people normally do not talk, and we even ask survey questions in a language that is not commonly spoken by the average person. I believe that humanizing business practices and translating them to everyday life situations will make it easy for us to see how customers feel about them.

People do not always act the same way, as life situations influence each of us to a different extent. A teenager minutes before a final exam is not in the same mind-set he will be in right after the last final exam of the semester. In the same way, a successful corporate woman has different mind-sets at different times. Her mind-set when she is getting ready for work in the morning is not the same as her mind-set when she is walking into a staff meeting later in the day. It is not the same as her mind-set when she is at a networking happy hour, and of course, it is not the same as her mind-set when she is simply sitting down at home after returning from a long day at work or when she is at a beach on vacation. Hence, every person can be in different mind-sets based on life situations, and the relationship partner should be aware of the mind-set to best communicate with that person. Looking at the example of the corporate woman, her boyfriend cannot have the same conversation with her in each of the above situations. Let me build a fun matrix to determine how she will react to different conversations in each of the different situations.

Situation	Right Time to Say	May Not Be the Right Time to Say
Getting ready for work in the morning	"I love you. I just wanted to say that. Good luck with the presentation. You will wow everyone at the office today."	"Did you make the reservation for the Broadway show?"
Walking into a staff meeting	"I got your laptop fixed and will drop it at your office before the end of the day."	"I found the perfect church for us to get married in. You will love it."
Socializing at a networking happy hour	"I am stuck in Chicago because of bad weather. I will keep you posted as I find out more."	"Tomorrow morning, can you pick up the laundry and bring it to work? I am going on a business trip straight from work."
Sitting down at home after returning from a long day at work	"How was your day? How was the presentation? Can I get you a cup of your favorite tea?"	"We should talk about a few things we can do to improve our relationship."
Lying on a beach on vacation	"You look beautiful. I am so glad I am here with you."	"What is your career plan for the next five years?"

The different reactions to the same person in different situations work the same way in the business world. The same customer is in a different mind-set when he is at a store looking for replacement batteries for his wristwatch compared to when he is there on the weekend with his wife and kids. A college student is in a different mind-set when he stops in a restaurant to pick up a quick lunch versus when he is there with his friends over the weekend. I have been observing customer behavior for the last thirty years, and based on the influence of all the different mind-sets, I have arrived at the conclusion that customers are in one of two different mind-sets. I describe the mind-sets as the butterfly mind-set and the terminator mind-set. Please note that I am not calling a customer a butterfly or a terminator, as even though each customer might have a natural tendency to align with one mind-set more than the other, he or she will switch from one mind-set to the other as the situation he or she is in changes. Here is a description of each mind-set.

The Butterfly Mind-Set

A customer is in a butterfly mind-set when he or she is in no immediate rush. He or she is present in the moment and open to a lighthearted conversation. Here are a few typical everyday butterfly situations for customers.

- At an upscale restaurant, while getting ready to order a glass of wine, he wants to know what the server's favorite wines are. He also wants to discover the best wines the restaurant offers that guests order rarely.
- At an electronics store, he starts a discussion about different televisions to understand their impact on the environment.
- At a home improvement store, he asks about types of roses and which ones will grow best in that location.
- At a department store, she is browsing through a new line of purses and looking at the mirror, holding each one.
- At a fast food restaurant, he is looking at the menu and trying to get an idea of what he feels like eating today.
- At a car dealership, she is looking for replacement batteries and wants to understand the differences in the guarantees of various batteries.
- On an online site, he is searching for a golf gift, and he texts a buddy about the search results.
- On an online movie site, he is browsing new releases to decide what his family will enjoy watching that night.

In each of the above situations, the customer is in a nonurgent mode and seeking information at his or her pace. These customers want to be engaged in a conversation. They are ready to listen, learn, and process information. In short, they have a need or purpose that is not critical and is not yet clear to them. They are ready to be guided in a relaxed way to fine-tune their needs.

The Terminator Mind-Set

Think about the 1984 movie *Terminator* by Orion Pictures. In that movie, when the Terminator seeks something, his computerized vision focuses clearly on what he wants. He does not want an interruption or distraction. The same mind-set can be seen in a customer who clearly knows what he or she wants. Here are a few typical everyday terminator situations for customers in each of the businesses mentioned in the previous example.

- At an upscale restaurant, she asks if the food the server brought to the table has peanuts, as the customer has a peanut allergy.
- At an electronics store, he asks if they can fix his big-screen television.
- At a home improvement store, he asks if they can match the paint in his bedroom.
- At a department store, he is looking for a specific brand of jeans in his exact size.
- At a fast food restaurant, he asks if he left his keys there earlier that day.
- At a car dealership, he is looking for replacement batteries for his remote car key.
- On an online shopping site, she is searching for a left-handed golf driver from a certain brand.
- On an online movie site, she is trying to find a specific movie.

In each of the above situations, the customer is in a mode different from the butterfly mode. A customer in a terminator mode knows what he or she wants and does not want. These customers do not want to be engaged in a conversation; they want clear yes-or-no answers. In short, they have a definite need that must be fulfilled before they do anything else.

Every employee must be aware of the customer's mind-set when he or she interacts with that customer. A butterfly customer needs unrushed attention. The employee must listen to the customer and confirm that he or she is at the best place to fulfill his or her needs. The employee should provide the customer with answers to his or her questions in a converging way. Converging answers help the customer close in on a purchase decision, as opposed to diverging answers, which open up new questions in the customer's mind.

Contrastingly, a terminator customer needs a direct answer to his or her query. Here are some examples of responses a terminator customer would like to receive: "No, sir, we do not carry it, but do you want me to see if I can have it shipped directly to you for free?" or "I know exactly what you are looking for. Let me walk you to the right section of the store." A complete "Whoa!" from a terminator customer will come if the employee tells him, "We do not have the jeans that you are looking for. However, we have other styles in the men's section over there," or "Too bad your television isn't working. Why fix it, when you can buy a new one? Let us walk to the television section, and I can help you find a good deal."

At the center of defining a mind-set as butterfly or terminator are two core concepts that are becoming more and more important in defining customer expectations from any business. They are pacing and control, specifically being self-paced and being in control. Together, both concepts determine whether a customer will be in a butterfly or terminator mind-set. Being self-paced defines a customer's need to move at his or her speed. He or she does not want to be rushed. Being in control refers to the customer not feeling coerced into something. Visualize a highway with two separate lanes. Based on the self-paced concept, lane one is for customers who drive at their pace. In this lane, there is no minimum speed limit, and it is okay to stop anytime. In lane two, everyone simply whooshes by, as they are all in a hurry to get somewhere. Based on the being-in-control concept, the customer has complete choice of where he or she drives. He or she can go in lane one today and lane two tomorrow or the other way around. The customer can switch lanes any time and as often as he or she wishes, which means the customer can switch between a butterfly and a terminator state, and every time, he or she expects the employee to change his or her response accordingly.

The two mind-sets are relevant in dating too. Most dates start with both persons in the butterfly mind-set. But if some situation changes, then one or both turn into terminators. Here are a few examples of situation changes that are surely going to bring one or both into a terminator mind-set.

- One of them gets a text that the babysitter has a family emergency and has to leave soon.
- They learn that a big storm changed its direction and is coming straight in their direction.
- They were planning to go to a movie after their date, and they just learned that tickets are available for an earlier show in a theater not far from the restaurant.

The server in the restaurant was pampering the two customers in their butterfly mind-set. As one or both changes to the terminator mind-set, the server too needs to switch service mode to befit a terminator. He or she might have to rush to get the check and pack the food, making it easy for the customers to leave immediately.

In an ideal situation, every team member should be able to read minds, the same way every person in a relationship would find it helpful to read minds. That might be asking a lot, as reading minds takes a lot of training. Instead, businesses should encourage team members to be more aware of their customers. Team members should pay attention to not only what the customer is asking for but also how he or she is asking. This way, all team members will feel empowered to take time and be attentive and will be ready to switch the responses they provide.

Understanding Relationships

Relationships are manifestations of how humans interact with each other. In order for a relationship to have any chance of becoming meaningful, a person has to first invest in the relationship. That is the karma of a relationship: you only get back what you put in. In the same way, if a brand believes in good karma, shouldn't it start by being genuinely interested in a customer? The more interested the brand is in the customer, the more likely it is that the customer will reward the brand by showing interest in the brand.

As a brand strives to build a strong connection with its customers, it must remember that relationships have phases. A deeper understanding of the phases will shed more light on how business relationships evolve.

Understanding why we get into relationships and how relationships evolve is important in order for brands to realize why a customer will choose to build a long-term relationship with them. A journey

must start with self-discovery. Before jumping into the dating world and seeking a relationship, it is always important to have a clear idea of who one is and what one is seeking.

Here Are the Four Relationship Phases of a Date

1. **First Impression:** Within seconds of the start of a date, one forms a first impression that sets the tone for the rest of the date. Doesn't the same thing happen within minutes of entering a new store that one is visiting for the first time? The first impression is important in building a relationship.
2. **Making It Easy to Explore:** This is the early part of the date. During this phase, both individuals are cautious and simply want to explore. The same thing happens with a first visit to a store, as the customer in this phase wants to walk around and let the surroundings soak in.
3. **Seeking Confirmation:** As the date progresses, both persons become aware of a reality. The reality is that at the end of the date, each has to decide if there is going to be a second date. Hence, they start becoming a little more proactive in getting information they need for this decision.
4. **The Grand Finale: Decision Time:** At the end of the date, each person makes a decision about the future of the connection. A customer goes through exactly the same emotions during the first visit to the store.

As we go through the phases of customer karma, it is important to know that the focus should not be only on doing good karma always. How and when you do good karma also matter. Good karma should be done in a spontaneous, natural way without the other person feeling stressed or overwhelmed.

Humanizing Customer Relationships

The business world is all about relationships and shared experiences; these include relationships with customers and internal relationships with team members. It might be beneficial to get a broader understanding of how human relationships work. Let me start by focusing on how a romantic relationship between two people starts. This learning might provide insight into how a brand can start a relationship with an individual. One of the key starting points is a date. For a typical date, the outline should be as follows:

- The man has information about the potential date. The information could have come from an online connection that caught his eye, an introduction by a friend, or an encounter at a social gathering.
- Based on the information, he has a perception of her in his mind. The perception has to be positive for him to be interested in her.
- As he thinks more about her, he gets more intrigued by her, and at some point, his interest in her turns into a desire, and he wants to meet and get to know her. That is the point when he decides to ask her out.
- Assuming she agrees to go out with him, they go out on a date. He is curious and excited but, at the same time, a little unsure. The curiousness and excitement come from the positive perception he has of her in his mind. His uncertainty stems from the fact that he knows that a lot of people glorify their profiles on dating sites, or friends often exaggerate about someone they are trying to set you up with, and in both cases, the perceptions fall flat in real life. These thoughts and feelings create expectations and doubt that he carries with him into the first date.

Interest, Desire, and Action in Dating

have thought a date was simply a man or a woman asking someone out, but you must realize the sequence of information processing and decision making that occurs to make the date happen. The dating process parallels the classic, age-old marketing concept of awareness, interest, desire, and action (AIDA). There is no clear inventor of this concept, but the term and approach are commonly attributed to American advertising and sales pioneer E. St. Elmo Lewis.[2] The AIDA concept states that a customer needs to be first aware of the product. No customer has ever bought a product that he or she was not aware of. After the customer is aware of the product, that awareness creates an interest in the product. The interest starts growing and makes the customer want the product, and finally, once the desire gets strong, it leads him or her to take action to buy the product.

A customer's experience with a product follows the outline below.

- The customer becomes aware of a new product. An advertisement of the product or word of mouth might be the source of awareness.
- Based on the content of awareness, he or she has a perception of the product in his or her mind. That perception results in the customer's interest in the product.
- Over time, the interest evolves, and his or her level of desire for the product increases.
- Once the desire for the product crosses a threshold, the customer acts on it and buys the product.

Just as in the dating example, in this case too, the customer is curious and excited but a little unsure. The curiousness and excitement come from his or her interest in and desire for the product. The lack of certainty stems from the fact that he or she knows that brands sometimes set expectations that are a little exaggerated, just like dating pictures. The customer has learned that a frozen entrée never looks like the picture on the package after microwaving, a fast-food sandwich rarely looks like the picture on the print advertising, and he or she never looks as cool as the advertisement when he or she wears a newly purchased sweater. Of course, the customer is being lighthearted in the last example, as he or she blames the model in the print advertising for being misleading.

If you reflect on the dating example, you will see that for every first date to happen, a person has to go through the awareness, interest, desire, and action phases. Because both dating and the customer experience follow the AIDA concept, we can establish that there is a parallel between dating and the customer experience. I wanted to showcase that before getting into the content of the book. You will see me repeating the comparison, as I feel personalizing this information and looking at it from a dating perspective as well as a business perspective will make it easier to understand how our actions impact the customer.

Consider this: in the dating world, one does not put a limited-time-offer coupon next to his or her profile picture to get more dates. That would make a person look strange and desperate. Then why do brands do this every day to get customers? The reason is that many times, a large number of people go to a retail outlet to buy a product that is being advertised at a special price. Once someone is in the store, he or she might realize that the store is out of the product, and in that case, a clerk might give him or her a rain check. The giving of a rain check has become such an acceptable practice that hardly anyone acknowledges the inconvenience and disappointment caused to the customer. A direct analogy of this in the dating example would be for a date to not show up. Imagine that when a woman gets to the restaurant, she gets a text from her date saying that he cannot make it today but promises a follow-up date the next week. In the dating example, you will be able to feel the pain and disappointment of the person a lot more than in the rain check example. Even though her date said he was sorry, she is disappointed. She has been looking forward to this for the last few days, and she had to plan around work and life events to be able to make it. As she drives home, she thinks, *This is not fair.* The negative impact of the no-show on the person is a lot more apparent in the dating example. Hence, instead of talking about our business practices and making this a formal business book, I will use the analogy of dating. I also think it will be a more fun book to write, and I am sure you will enjoy reading this book. Who knows? I might be writing one of the best sellers among the how-to-go-on-better-dates books!

A Journey Must Start with Self-Discovery

As I said, good karma in a relationship starts with one investing in the relationship first, and investment must be from the heart. Hence, it is essential for a person to have a clear idea of who he or she is. Before one jumps into the dating world seeking a relationship, it is always important to have a clear idea of who one is and what one is seeking. I believe this must happen even before the person takes any steps in the dating world. Self-discovery involves big-picture thinking and happens when there is no rush, urgency, or pressure to succeed.

Proper self-discovery takes sincerity and honesty, as accepting oneself for who he or she is makes a person feel confident. This process results in setting the right expectations for the first date and allowing one to be comfortable in all of his or her interactions with dates. Not setting the right expectations for the first date might result in the date starting with one's dating partner thinking, *What the heck am I doing here?* Along with this, having clarity about whom you want to go out with ensures that you end up on dates that you feel have a high chance of success.

What Is Common among a Coffee Shop, a Sports Beverage, a Theme Park, and a Hair Dresser?

Now let me review how a brand's self-discovery works in the corporate world. The self-discovery for a brand involves having a clear idea of what the brand offers. A national coffee brand does not just sell coffee, a sports drink company sells more than a beverage, guests do not go to a theme park just to go on rides, and a haircut place does more than simply cut people's hair. Let's look at these four examples in more depth.

- What does a national coffee brand offer? If the customer thinks the brand offers just coffee, then the customer will not pay five dollars for a cup of coffee. Instead of just a cup of coffee, the customer gets a much-sought-after break and an opportunity to recharge during his or her day. The authentic coffee aroma when one walks in; all the coffee equipment in the store, which shows authenticity; the dedicated coffee barista who makes the coffee one cup at a time; and the professional businesspeople hanging out in the coffee shop all add to the experience of the product. Hence, when a national fast-food place tries to enter the space and compete simply by adding similar coffee to their menu, somehow, that does not connect with the customer. The fast-food brand must understand that the customer wants more than coffee.

- What does a sports drink company sell? A sports beverage company does not simply quench thirst during sporting events. Instead, it sells a hope that drinking the beverage will make the person connect with the sports personality endorsing the product and think that he or she can be as successful as a sports personality by drinking the product. Hence, the sports drink sells dreams and implied but not guaranteed promises. A great example of this is Gatorade's 1991 television advertisement featuring the "Be like Mike" jingle, a catchy song that made every young sports fan connect to Michael Jordan's passion and style of winning. The "Be like Mike" jingle clearly touched on every sports fan's desire and dream to be like Michael Jordan. Even though the ad never made the promise that by drinking Gatorade, one would become like Michael, Gatorade was presented as an integral part of Michael's journey to success. Hence, if a sports fan was dreaming of becoming like Mike, he or she would dream with a Gatorade bottle in his or her hand. Based on the ad, Gatorade became the sports drink most relevant to sports fans at that time.

- What does a theme park offer? A visit to a theme park creates a lifetime of memories for a guest. The memories are more enduring than any of the temporary rides or activities. The experience is about not just the rides but also the anticipation of going to the park with friends, the speculation on how each person will react to different rides, and the pictures to post on social media with captions about each other's screaming during the rides. In a way, the theme park gets the friends together and creates moments when each of them can be his or her own self. That creates authentic memories that make the trip to the theme park worth it.

- Finally, does a haircut place offer more than just haircuts? For all my male friends, I ask you to think about what happens at the end of a haircut. The stylist holds a mirror at different angles to show a man how the back of his hair looks. Do most men care about how the backs of their heads look? I do not think so. Instead, the holding of the mirror makes most men feel special, and they leave the haircut place feeling cool and fashionable. A haircut is a promise of a more successful return to the personal and professional world. It might lead to more self-confidence, as after the haircut, one might see himself as sharp and ready to take on the world.

Why is this self-discovery important before one takes any steps in the dating world? Unless people know themselves and have some clarity on what they are seeking, they will meet anyone with whom they can relate. They leave meeting the right person to chance. It is similar to someone planning a trip without knowing where he or she is or is going.

In the same way, it is important for a brand to understand what a brand sells, as without that understanding, the company will only be a coffee-distribution business and not a coffee-experience business. Employees must clearly understand the business they are in. You do not want coffee-experience-business employees to act as if they are in the coffee-distribution business. If they act as if they are in the coffee-distribution business, their favorite word will be *next* after they hand over the coffee cups. Over time, they can be replaced by a vending machine that will provide the same consistent coffee every time. I do not know about you, but I am not going to pay five dollars for coffee from a vending machine. You might call me insecure, but to pay five dollars, I need a smile to greet me, and I need someone to put some TLC in my coffee and then give it to me with a sincere wish of "Have a great day." The visit to the coffee store makes me feel good, and I am okay with spending five dollars for it.

Start Strong

Within seconds of the start of a date, you put the other person into one of three buckets.

1. Extreme negative: "What I am doing out with him?"
2. Extreme positive: "Wow, I am lucky to be out with him."
3. Undecided: "Hmm. Let me see how it goes."

Doesn't the same thing happen within minutes of entering a new store that you are visiting for the first time? This is the beginning of good karma in a relationship. If you start with good karma and have a positive halo, you will have a good start in your relationship.

Just like on a date, the power of the first impression can be a deal maker or breaker in a customer's experience. The critical thing to remember is that the first impression blends the first few elements of a customer's experience with his or her past knowledge, stereotypes, and beliefs. The combination of elements creates the first impression. Based on that, the first reaction happens. As past knowledge, stereotypes, and beliefs in the customer's mind are strong, it is essential that the first few elements of a customer's experience be impactful and define the reaction. Ideally, the first impression should do one of the following.

- It should challenge the customer's way of thinking. In this case, the store would be saying, "You were not sure if this store has a place in your life. Now you know it is something you clearly want to explore. You truly did not know something like this existed."
- It should confirm what the customer already knew but position the new brand as a better alternative. In this case, the store would be saying, "You have used similar brands in the past, but we clearly

are a step above. We have worked hard to understand what you need, and our knowledge and efforts show. Please explore, as we are sure you will see that what we offer has a better fit in your life."

In the same way, the first reaction on a date is a blend of what your date already knows about you, is expecting, and has experienced on past dates and the first few seconds of interaction. Here are a few examples of different ways you could start a date and the resulting first impression.

Your First Interaction	Resultant First Impression
You walk in, still on the phone. You smile at your date and make a pleading face, implying that it will take just a few more minutes to finish the call.	She feels ignored and not important. She feels you are too busy to have a meaningful social life.
You walk in, sit down, and place the phone on the table in front of you.	She feels she is on a timer, or you are expecting calls that are more important than talking to her. She feels that if the phone rings, you will pause the date and answer the phone.
You walk in with a bouquet of lilies.	It is a moment that will make her say, "Aww." She is happy, as she told you on the phone that she loves lilies and not roses. She is impressed that you listened.
Your date walks into a quiet restaurant that you chose. It is local, and it is different; it is something you are sure your date will like based on the phone conversation you had with her.	She is impressed that you listened to the fact that she does not like chain restaurants and that you researched to find the perfect restaurant for the two of you.
You text her an hour before the date to say that you have to end the date at eight o'clock, as you have to leave for the airport to pick up a friend. You thank her for being understanding and say you are looking forward to the date.	The date has not yet begun, and you are planning the end. That might not come across as a positive first impression.

You and your date are driving separately. She follows you to the parking lot. You see an open spot right in front of the door. Instead of taking it, you pass it and wave your hands to her to make sure she notices the spot.	This is a nice gesture of kindness and thoughtfulness and will be sure to result in a positive first impression.

In the world of customer experience, the first impression happens exactly the same way. The table below gives examples of different first impressions created by brands.

Situation, including Customer's Past Knowledge, Stereotypes, and Beliefs	Brand Input	The Customer's First Impression
The customer is scared of dental work. He thinks it is painful, and recovery takes a long time.	The customer walks into the waiting area. Incoming patients are sitting on the left side. On the right side are patients who are recovering after their dental procedures.	The customer sees the patients who have gone through the procedures and looks at the swollen faces. That visual reinforces that the experience will be painful. He knows for sure this will be a painful adventure.
	The receptionist greets the customer and gives him the paperwork. On top of the paperwork is a printed television guide for the next hour. The receptionist draws attention to it and says that the customer can choose what he wants to watch as the dentist goes through the procedure.	This information is something the customer did not expect. He thinks, *Hmm, I can watch television as the dentist does the procedure? That is interesting. I guess it is not going to hurt that much.*

The customer is buying a phone and feels that he is somewhat technologically challenged.	The store employee hands him the phone and says, "Please make sure you read the entire user manual before you start using the phone. There is an online link for additional information. That link will also give you access to chat help should you need it."	The customer is convinced that it will not be easy to use the phone. He feels he will have to spend a few hours studying the manual, and then maybe he will be online for a few hours before he can make the first phone call using his new phone. He worries that he might feel stupid after buying the phone, as it will be a challenge to make the first phone call.
	The store employee finds an open table in the store and invites the customer to come sit there. The store employee then asks for the current phone and starts the transfer process to the new phone. As he does it, he keeps sharing some of the cool features of the new phone. Then he asks the customer whom he wants to make his first call to and helps him make the first call and experience all the cool features firsthand.	The customer is excited. He feels like a little kid and knows that soon he will have his new phone and be ready to make calls. He is excited to explore the new features. He starts sharing during his first call how much he loves the phone. Within minutes of the purchase, he has become a brand messenger for the phone.

The customer comes to a sit-down restaurant during lunch. As he stands outside, he is worried it might take too long to eat lunch there.	The customer sees from outside that people are standing near the counter. It seems that there is a long wait.	The customer feels that this restaurant is not suitable for a quick lunch, and he might consider using it later, on a day when he has a lot more time.
	The customer walks in and sees an iPad on the table. The iPad has a menu, and there is a description of each menu item, as well as a price and an estimate of how long it will take the server to bring the food to him.	The customer is assured that he will be fine with his time. He is in control. He can order what he wants and pay on the iPad when he finishes eating.

Often, businesses get too caught up in serving customers who are already in the store and forget to pay attention to guests who have just walked in. When a guest walks in and does not know where to go or what to do next, it is similar to going to a party and not being sure if you belong there. It is important to be attentive to the guest and create a positive first impression. However, attentiveness does not mean the store employee screams from the counter, "Welcome to the store! I will get to you when I am free." The first impression must be personal; it must make the guest feel assured, welcome, and excited about what lies ahead. First impressions are the first step in establishing lifelong relationships. To truly understand the impact of the first impression, simply humanize it by using the dating example, and you will immediately feel the joy or the pain the customer experiences.

Making It Easy to Explore

After a good first impression, customers move to an exploration mode, which comes out of curiosity when the customer has developed an interest for the product. Brands need to create an environment to invite the exploratory spirit of customers by making them feel comfortable to explore. Exploring is different for different customers and, hence, is self-paced, just like the butterfly customer mind-set I discussed earlier. A butterfly customer simply enjoys the exploration.

You Are Simply Taking Too Long

The exploration can happen either in the digital world or in the physical world. In the physical world, when a customer enters a retail store, the first impression must be strong enough to trigger a desire to explore. Once he or she starts exploring, team members should be available if the customer has questions, but saying to the customer every few minutes, "What are you looking for? Maybe I can help," does not create a free environment to explore. It rushes the customer and makes the customer feel that the employee is saying, "You are taking too long." The same applies when a customer comes to a website. Within seconds, the customer must feel that he or she is at the right place, as otherwise, the customer will click on the next site. As it is much easier to leave the site compared to a physical store location, the first impression is even more important in this case. Thus, the site should be designed in a way that the customer feels comfortable and confident to explore at his or her own pace. It is good to have access to chat support, but if the chat bubble starts opening up every few seconds, it interrupts the natural exploration. The site must be confident that the customer will be able to find the support and use it if needed. In both examples, it is essential to create an environment conducive to exploration. Encourage the customers, and give them time and space, but be there when they need any help. Just know that only after the customer explores on his or her terms does interest turn into desire. Then the customer wants the product. Brands should realize that brand perceptions developed as a result of a customer's self-discovery are way more powerful than the perception created based on forced communication.

In the dating example, this phase often does not have a lot of spoken words. Your date might be quiet, taking a sip of the wine and smiling at you as both of you sit at the table. She might be processing everything in her mind. The initial anxiety is over. She is getting comfortable to start a conversation. As she takes her time, please do not feel pressured if her exploration style is more laid back. Do not interrupt her by saying, "You know, you can ask me any question on the planet. I am ready." That statement might ruin the moment and make your date feel that you are uncomfortable in her presence. Remind yourself that this is an emotional phase and, hence, does not require rational intervention. Simply let your date enjoy the moment, and your comfort in the present will create a free environment where she can ask what she wants to know at the right time. In the same way, when a customer takes baby steps to start cautiously exploring your brand, be excited that the customer is taking an interest in your store. Just like in the brand example, on a date, the things your date notices about you on her own are more powerful in deciding her perception of you than things you tell her about yourself.

Fun with Sauces in a Mexican Restaurant

As I was consulting with a Mexican fast-casual restaurant, the owners were perplexed about one big challenge. They offered different varieties of sauces and proudly displayed the sauces in the restaurant. The sauces were a perfect addition to the meal, allowing guests to customize each meal their way. There was one problem: hardly any customers were using the sauces.

As I looked around the restaurant, I saw the sauce collection. The sauces were all organized on a shelf, in ascending order of spiciness. There was a glass door on the shelf. The restaurant had built the sauce display with a lot of class and taste. As I stared at the sauces behind the glass, the glass made me feel as if the shelf were a display and not for me to touch. It was similar to going to a friend's place and looking at his wine collection in the cabinet. The wine I would open is the bottle he has placed on the table or the counter next to the meal. In the case of the restaurant, customers felt they did not have permission to explore the sauces. Once we got the sauce free from the display and created a sauce station where customers could be creative in mixing sauces, the usage of sauces increased immediately.

If You Don't Let Me Play with the Toys, It's No Fun

Similarly, in retail, some brands like to keep things behind glass doors or inside glass displays, or they lock them up so that you cannot check the products out without a store employee helping you. It is understandable for a store to protect certain products, such as expensive jewelry and watches. But what is the reason for putting headphones in a locked display? With technology, there are different ways to deter shoplifting, but stores should not implement processes that are a barrier to customer exploration, as barriers to exploration hinder the growth of the relationship with the customer.

Brands must understand that customers, especially when they are in a butterfly state of mind, like to take time to explore at their own pace. What customers learn on their own stays with them, and there's a high probability they'll share it through social media. Rushing the customer through this phase gets him or her to a transactional state where the customer is forced to make the following decisions.

1. Does this store have what I need?
2. Is this store better than my current solutions?
3. Is there anything I need to buy on this trip?
4. Is it time I leave the store?

The customer makes these decisions based on his or her perception of the brand and not on facts. This illustrates why the perception of the brand in the customer's mind is important and why brands need to give customers all the time they need to build their perceptions on their terms.

Seeking Confirmation

As a date evolves from the exploration phase to the confirmation phase, the date arrives at a defining phase. It is important to realize that the date is no longer in an emotional phase; it is in more of an objective phase.

As I mentioned earlier, by now, the impressing-each-other-stories are over. The conversation slows down, and there are more pauses than before. Each person uses this phase to ask questions to find out what he or she wants to know instead of what the other person wants to share. In this phase, each person tries to find the missing pieces of a puzzle so that he or she can create a complete picture of the other. This digging for information happens cautiously and often through indirect questions. Both are hesitant to be too direct with their questions, but they both realize that the fuller the picture one has of the other, the better the chance he or she has to make an informed decision about the future of this connection. Hence, there is a balancing game. One does not want to come across as being too forward with his or her questions. At the same time, if this connection has no future, both parties want to know that on this date and not after two or three dates.

Common questions in this phase include questions about what a person likes to do in his or her free time (is the person a laid-back person or someone who must be out with friends on Friday?); one's beliefs in life; and, if one has kids, the role a partner would play in the kids' lives. As you can see, the questions in this phase are heavier and deeper than before. Hence, there is more responsibility to make it comfortable for the other person to ask these questions. The person asking the questions has to be responsible for seeing how the natural progression of the questions has gone before asking a new question.

Here are a few example questions and statements and how they might define the perception.

- **What are your religious beliefs?** If the person asking the questions starts with "What are your religious beliefs?" it is surely going to startle the other person. Let's say a woman asks her date this right away. The asking of the question itself might make the other person feel that his date is religious and that strong alignment of religious beliefs is important to her for a connection. This perception of his date will define the future of the date, and his date might never get a chance to explain that she asked the question because she is not rigid in her religious belief.
- **I am not comfortable talking about it.** If the answer to a question about religious beliefs or another question is an abrupt "I am not comfortable talking about it," that could be followed by a deadly silence, and the question could eventually be a DEM (date-ending move). The silence tells the other person she has asked a question that is inappropriate and has come across as judgmental. One does not have to share his religious beliefs unless he is ready to share them. He might defer the discussion by saying, "That question has a lot of different facets. I have been influenced by my religion and by how my parents raised me. As I cannot separate religion from what my parents taught me, it is a long discussion, and I am sure we will enjoy it on the next date."

Does Buying an Extended Warranty Mean the Product Will Stop Working Soon?

As customers go through the exploration phase, they must have a complete picture of the business's offering. If a customer is looking for an electronic gadget, he will want to ask, "How likely is it that this product will break down soon?" He might consider that an abrupt, rude question, or he might think that if he directly asks, he might not get a clear answer. But getting an idea of the answer is important to him. Hence, he might ask instead, "If I bought this product, how important do you think it is that I get an extended warranty?" The store team member must understand what the customer wants to find out and recognize that he is in need of assurance. The employee should not give an abrupt answer, such as "It is totally up to a customer to decide if he or she wants to buy an extended warranty." That answer will result in a silence similar to the answer "I am not comfortable talking about it." Instead, the employee needs to find different ways to assure the customer. For example, the clerk might say, "In the unlikely case that the product breaks down, we will stand behind the product. For the first year, if there are any problems, simply bring the product back, and we will take care of it in the store itself. You don't have to find ways of shipping the product for repair. After the first year, if there are any repairs, we have to charge you for materials and some labor costs. To avoid that possibility, some people buy the extended warranty. Hence, if you are planning to use this for a longer period, it is a smart decision to get the extended warranty, but let me assure you that you will not feel stranded if you don't get the extended warranty." In the long answer, the customer hears the employee's pride in the store, confidence, and assurance that the store will take care of customers in a fair and reasonable way. To me, that is a strong assurance, as the team member was transparent. How a warranty is presented to the customer can create doubt in the customer's mind or add assurance. Brands must be aware of this and not be desperate to make additional dollars by trying to sell an extended warranty.

Should We Order Salmon for Dinner?

In the corporate world, the word *transparent* is becoming more important every day. The influence of the millennial generation has brought transparency to the forefront. Millennial customers want transparency, but they are realistic and do not expect perfection. Here is an example that got me thinking. I was at a seafood restaurant, when the young couple sitting at the next table asked the server about the restaurant's sources for salmon. "Is it wild or farm raised?" they asked. It was clear that the couple knew their fish and had specific questions. The server answered, "By choice, we get farm-raised salmon only from select farms in Denmark and Norway. Even though many prefer wild caught, we have found that we cannot guarantee the quality in a wild-caught salmon. In a world where mercury poisoning is a possibility from seafood, we choose to get our salmon from two specific farms. Please know that we have direct access to information regarding how the salmon are raised on these farms. These farms don't have millions of salmon in a small tank like rush-hour traffic in Los Angeles. The farm has a rule on how many salmon can be in every one hundred cubic feet of water. The food the salmon get is 100 percent organic and controlled. The fish are also routinely tested to make sure they are disease-free." As the couple listened to the server, one of them was on her smartphone. I felt that she was checking out the information.

In this case, the two guests were in the confirmation phase of their experience at the restaurant. They were going through the menu and trying to learn about the restaurant's seafood sourcing policy. In this case, it was clear that the couple had walked in clearly preferring wild-caught salmon. The server could have given a short, clear answer, such as "Sorry, but our salmon is farm raised and not wild." That answer would have been sufficient for the guest, but the guest would not get to know the character of the restaurant. The transparent conversation from the server educated the couple. I want to point out a few things in the server's response that impressed me. He knew his facts and delivered the information with a lot of confidence. He also demonstrated that he was proud to work for the restaurant. At no point did he start an argument with the guests that the salmon in the restaurant was better than what the guests had had before. He made the information available and then left the guests free to decide what they wanted. He did more than talk about salmon. He defined the restaurant's personality and practices. He showed that the restaurant cares about the food it serves and has strict standards. The restaurant also hires quality employees who are trained to deliver the information in detail to the guests. The server's response is similar to the response of the employee at the electronics store. Both responses have a tone similar to the date's answer on religion. In all three cases, an abrupt one-liner would have prevented the relationship from moving forward.

At the end of the date, each person has one of the following reactions:

1. Positive: "I really want to go out with him again. I hope he feels the same way."
2. Negative: "Nope, never, not even if he were the last man on earth."
3. Undecided: "Hmm, I'm not sure. Maybe we can catch a movie sometime."

During the first visit to the store, a customer goes through exactly the same emotions. At the end of the visit, the customer categorizes the store in one of the following ways: "This is one of my favorites," "This is not for me," or "I will keep it in mind." All the confirmation a customer can get before making the decision increases the probability of a relationship evolving with the customer.

The Grand Finale: Decision Time

The endgame is the area where there is one big difference between a date and a customer interaction. On a date, each person evaluates if he or she wants to go out with the other person, and only if both individuals want to go out together is there a follow-up date. When each realizes that the other person is interested in him or her, it creates excitement. Remember, when they walked in, they were excited, but excitement in this phase is different, as individuals exchange pleasantries and appreciations. Each feels good to have found the other person, and genuineness and sincerity define the exchange. But in the world of customer interaction, the endgame is often the most overlooked part of the guest experience, primarily because the decision is only with the customer. Often, brands have not acknowledged the fact the customer sits in their store and decides in their presence how to use the brand in the future. Brands have tremendous opportunities to influence the decision. Here are a few examples of the grand finale in the customer experience.

Postdinner Restless Syndrome Spreading in Restaurants

You and your significant other are dining out at an exclusive restaurant. The service was outstanding; the food was great; and as you finish the last spoonful of dessert, you are ready to leave. You get restless as you try to make eye contact with the server so that you can signal that you are ready for the check. You want to pay and then start driving toward home. Unfortunately, the server, who was constantly at the table earlier, asking if everything was okay, if you wanted another glass of wine, or if you had left room for dessert, is now tough to spot. As you get restless, you realize that you are not in control of the situation anymore. You start feeling less special, and with every second, the specialness of the experience starts eroding. Put this situation in perspective by thinking of the following date scenario. As both of you are ready to leave, your date leaves the table to have a conversation with friends at a different table. It starts as a harmless gesture, but after some time, you start to get irritated, as you have no idea how long it will be before she returns. When she finally returns, there could well be an awkward silence. As both of you walk out of the restaurant, the awkwardness defines the experience and overshadows all of the cool moments of the date.

What could the server do to make the end of the dining experience special? Imagine that the experience went this way. During the dinner, the server was aware that you were in a butterfly mind-set. After he brought the dessert to the table, he was aware of your mind-set. The moment he saw that your mind-set changed to that of a terminator, he brought the check. As he placed the check in the leather check holder, he thanked you and said, "If you give me your valet number, I can get your car pulled as you are paying. You can also put your tip for the valet in the holder, and I will make sure he gets it. This way, you do not have to wait outside the restaurant at all." Wow! Instead of making you wait, he saved you time at the valet. That must have made you feel great about the restaurant as you left.

Final Moment at a Resort

You spent three nights at an exclusive resort, and in the morning, you are planning to check out of the hotel. You wake up, and the first thing you see is that the detailed statement for your stay has been printed and pushed under the door. Unlike with the restaurant experience, here, the check is given to you even before you asked for it. But is this the last interaction you want with the resort? Does it make you feel that you are in a completely transactional relationship? The impersonal delivery of the invoice is bound to erase some of the service moments you experienced during your stay.

What could the resort do to make the end special? Let me take a step back and go through your experience, starting when you came in. The room was clean, and everything was in place. There was a welcome note from the employee who had personally gotten the room ready for you. Based on your personal profile, the hotel had put the right kind of pillow and an extra blanket in the room. As a final touch, there were two mints on the pillows. Should an experience that started with so much personal attention finish with an invoice pushed under the door when you are leaving? To me, this would be comparable to one's date leaving in the middle of the night, when he was sleeping, and leaving a note on the table. In the note, she wrote how much both of you had spent during the last few days, how much she had paid, and how much she owed you. That would change the tone of the entire experience. Instead, what if she left a cute note stating how much she hated to leave but explaining that she had to catch an early-morning flight and did not want to disturb you by waking you up? That note, with a little more intimate personalization, would put a big smile on your face. Now that I have humanized the resort experience, what could the resort do to put a smile on your face? Shouldn't the final connection with the resort be a personal handwritten note from the resort's manager, thanking you? What if he enclosed his business card and insisted that you call him directly for all future stays at the resort?

Credit Card Push at a Department Store

You are at a department store's checkout. The cashier shares with you that you can save 10 percent of the entire amount by signing up for the store's credit card. You politely refuse, but the cashier keeps insisting. You have a déjà vu moment, as this has happened the last three times you visited the store. You were hoping that by now, they would have marked in their database that you are not interested in signing up for the credit card and that they should not try to sell you the credit card every time. Instead, it looks as if the store believes that you are ready to give in, as if one last effort will make you sign up for the credit card. The insistence of the store to sell the credit card might be the equivalent of a man insisting that his date come in for coffee or a drink after the date, when she has clearly indicated in the past that she is not ready for it. The first time he extended the offer, she got it that he liked her and wanted to spend more time with her. But asking her frequently if she is ready to take the relationship to the next level and making her say no after every date is not a pleasant experience for her.

What could the department store do to make the end special? To me, this one is simple. Once a customer says no at the checkout, the store should make a note that this customer does not want to be bothered by the credit card offering. With all the customer tracking that stores do using loyalty cards and customers' credit cards, this is something stores could easily pull off.

All I Want to Do Is Cancel My Cable Account

You are ready to cancel your cable subscription. You stay on hold for fifteen minutes to finally get to the operator. All you want is an assurance that effective that day, your cable is disconnected and the cable company has stopped charging you. Instead of processing this simple request, the operator starts explaining to you about new specials and keeps insisting that you should try them out. This example is similar to a situation in which your date calls you to tell you that she wants to break up with you. You should be classy and nice and make it easy for her to get her point through. You need to understand that it is not easy for her to have the conversation. Instead of making it easy for her, what if you start pleading for a second chance? You share with her the details of the perfect date you have planned for her this upcoming weekend and say she must try that before breaking up. Your behavior might come across as a seriously pathetic gesture, and no good karma can come out of that.

What could the cable operator do to make the end special? First, understand that the company missed their chance to impress you when you were still their customer. You might be leaving because of a bad customer experience. Instead of understanding that and giving you a forum to share your frustration, the operator is trying to overcome your bad experience with new specials, effectively telling you, "If you take these specials and stay, you will forget the bad experiences." Instead, the operator should listen and try to make your last call to the cable company uneventful and quick.

As these types of exchanges have become part of our everyday experiences with brands, I have started to think that these are not big deals anymore.

But once you put them in the perspective of the dating examples, you will realize that the awkwardness and discomfort truly have a negative impact on the customer. Even if the customer is not complaining, these negative moments play a role in defining the future of the relationship. It is important to remember that this last phase is one in which the customer decides emotionally but justifies rationally. A brand cannot expect to create favorable emotional reactions by finishing the experience in an awkward or uncomfortable way.

What's Your Hurry, Cowboy? Savor the Moment

As I established the four phases of a date, I put aside the concept of customer karma. Now let me bring it back and review with you how your actions during the date will fall into one of two buckets—good karma or bad karma—and how the net result of all karmas will impact the future of the relationship. It is not always about doing good karma; it is also about how you do good karma. Good karma should be done in a spontaneous, natural way without the other person feeling stressed or overwhelmed.

What is the purpose of the first date? It is simply to find out if there is a mutual connection and then get to a second date. Let me complicate this a little further. Think of a situation in which you want to go out with person A. You have been thinking about it for a while and finally ask her out. She says yes. Now, during either the first date or the second, you see this connection as a relationship that you want and start putting pressure on her to make a long-term commitment. It is likely that she will freak out, and your pressure tactics might make her walk away. To plan your preparation for the date, think of the purpose and goal of the first date. The purpose of the date is to be confident, get to know her, let her get to know you too, and hopefully decide together on a follow-up date. A long-term commitment comes into the picture only when both seek the same kind of commitment and not before that; it cannot be forced.

For those of you who are married with children, please go back in time and think about when you met your spouse for the first time. At the end of the first date, if you had told him or her the following, what would his or her reaction have been? "I am glad we went out today. But let me save us both a lot of time and come straight to the point. I see us dating for three years, during which there will be two trips together. As I know we are going to take the trips anyway, I have already booked the trips. This plan of mine will save us a lot of money, and we can plan ahead too. Then, in the fourth year, in early June, we will get married. I have short-listed two places where we can have our reception. That is not it. I also short-listed two hospitals where, three years after our marriage, we will have our first baby."

Unless your date thought you were really funny, he or she would have probably freaked out and walked out on you on that first date. The above statements are outrageous in the world of relationships, but in the business world, companies try hard to force a long-term commitment on the first date. Let me share with you a few examples.

Should I Become a Member of the Massage Spa?

First, let me talk about a national massage spa. Let's say you get a gift certificate and want to check it out. You book your first massage, and at the end of your massage, the person behind the counter pushes you to sign a contract. "You did enjoy the massage today, didn't you? A leading health study has shown that you should get a massage at least once a month. And what better way to commit to yourself than to join our preferred clients' massage club? Every month, you get as many massages as you want at the reduced price of fifty dollars each. Do you realize that without the club membership, you will be paying one hundred dollars for each massage?" As you listen to this sales speech, you are excited, as now you can get fifty-dollar massages—as many as you want. That is a great deal. As you get ready to fill out the form, the person behind the register adds, "And to make sure you get this offer, we need your credit card on file so we can autocharge you for a massage every month for the next two years. Think of it as your two-month commitment to yourself for massages." The words *credit card*, *autocharge*, and *two years* all wake you up. These words are similar to the phrases "vacation in the next two years," "marriage in the fourth year," and "first child in another three years" from the first date. Why can't the massage spa pause, take it easy, and only go for the second date? For example, the employee could say, "Here is an invite for two fifty-dollar massages for you that you can use in the next month. If you like these, then you should find out about the preferred clients' massage club program. But for now, enjoy the massages." This way, the massage spa would have made you aware of its interest in offering you a long-term relationship but given you the freedom to decide on it when and where you wanted to.

This desperation on the first date happens at other places too. Many retail outlets and department stores try to force you to sign up for their loyalty cards during the first purchase. As they try hard to get my e-mail address and cell phone number, I want to pause and remind them that in a dating situation, it is rude to ask for the e-mail address and cell phone number. The person shares that information when he or she is ready. Pressuring your date by asking repeatedly is similar to a child nagging and saying, "Why won't you give your contact information? Please, please, please!" Again, in the dating world, that behavior is not acceptable, but we are okay with it in the business world.

Anytime a store is trying to force me to make a commitment after the first interaction, I always go back to one of my favorite episodes of the CBS sitcom *The Big Bang Theory*. To show how close their friendship was, Raj gave Howard permission to remove the plastic film cover from Raj's new iPhone. As an excited Howard was trying to remove the plastic film cover in one pull, Raj paused him and made the classic statement "What's your hurry, cowboy? Savor the moment."

I feel this can be translated to the guest-experience example as "Yes, store, what's your hurry? Please give me some space and time. Trust me when I say that if and when I am ready to make a commitment, I will find you."

What could the massage spa have done to promote the contract in a positive way? I do not think there is anything wrong with teasing a customer with the benefits of the contract as long as the customer does not feel pressured to decide right now. What if the person behind the counter gives the receipt from the current visit in a jacket that talks about the contract and explains to the guest that he or she should seriously review the advantages of signing up as a member, as a member saves 33 percent on every massage? The employee might say, "Please do not feel rushed. You have four weeks from today to decide if you want to get the membership. In the meantime, if you have any questions, please feel free to call me. I would love to answer them." This would make the guest leave with a positive feeling regarding that day's experience and create a promise for future repeat occurrences, but with no pressure to decide immediately. This way of communicating shows the team member's confidence in the value of the massages and does not make him or her sound desperate to sell massage contracts.

There is another problem with rushing. Earlier, I talked about website and retail store examples where rushing can be annoying to the other person or the customer, but rushing can have some serious consequences for oneself too. When one is searching for a long-term relationship, he or she must give him- or herself enough time to get to know the person he or she is dating. Getting to know a person has both emotional and rational elements, and rushing through this phase often results in incomplete or improper perception. Hence, one should allow time for a complete picture of the other person to develop and not rush by using a partial picture, which results in false positives or false negatives. A false positive is when you find something positive and, based on that one factor, create an overall halo of positive that is not true. Similarly, a false negative happens when you find something negative and, based on that one factor, rush to a negative overall judgment. Let me share with you some simple examples.

Possible false positives include the following:

- We both like to watch basketball.
- I like the fact that she mostly wears red, which is my favorite color.
- We both are in similar professions.
- Both of us have the same all-time favorite movie.

In each of the above instances, there is evidence of an overlap in a like or shared interest. This evidence is encouraging and should drive both to spend more time getting to know each other rather than to come to a conclusion that there is an overall fit. That extreme stretching of the inference is a false positive.

Possible false negatives include the following:

- She is a morning person, and I am not.
- We have different taste in movies.
- She does not laugh at my jokes.
- She does not like to go out on weekdays.

In this set of instances, there is evidence of a difference in interests or habits. Of course, some differences in habits (e.g., one smokes and the other cannot tolerate smoking) can be deal breakers. But even if no one difference is a deal breaker, based on a few of these kinds of differences, one can extrapolate that this is not the right person for him or her. In this case, both need to act maturely and still get to know each other to see, despite the differences in interest and habits, what made them like each other after the first few dates.

Now let me translate this concept of false positives and false negatives to the world of customers. You must be wondering why it would be a problem for a brand to attract the wrong customer. Or you might be going a step further and asking, "How can there ever be a wrong customer?"

Can a Brand Ever Have a Wrong Customer?

Any consumer brand is defined by its users. When I was working on a project to identify how to increase traffic at a dance club, I learned clearly that not all dance clubs are for everyone. A person will only go to a dance club where people like him or her are likely to go. In this dance club, the DJ had mastered the science of music beats and their impact on different age groups. He proudly showed me how to plan music to decide who would be on the dance floor at any given time. He said he always started with the high beats, and that got the younger guests to the dance floor. He also explained to me that there was a maximum time the younger guests should be enjoying the high beats, as beyond that time frame, the group got irritated, and fights started to break out. As the cutoff time arrived, he switched gradually to slower beats, and there was a migration on the dance floor. The older guests would leave the bar and move to the dance floor, whereas the younger guests would move toward the bar to take a break. The older guests would be on the dance floor for a longer period than the younger guests, as they did not like to move from one place to another too fast. After I learned about this, I watched the DJ manage the different age groups of the guests effectively. What I learned from this experience was interesting.

- A guest only wants to be with those with similar interests.
- It is the business's responsibility to populate the business with similar guests if it wants the guest to feel comfortable at the place.

When I go to a coffee shop, I like the fact that it is filled with business professionals who are professionally dressed. I like to blend in and feel that I am part of the group. On the other hand, if the coffee shop were the destination for the high school football team after practice, I would not feel comfortable being there.

Hence, it is in the interest of both the guest and the business for the business to slow down and allow the guest to know the business at his or her pace. Patience is essential for a successful long-term relationship to grow.

Good Karma in Communication

Everyone is frustrated with lack of communication on this planet. Parents complain about children not listening; children, in turn, complain that parents have stopped listening. In a relationship, each partner complains that the other person does not listen. In the business world, customers complain that businesses do not listen to them when they have a problem, and businesses invest a sizable amount of resources to communicate with customers, as it is not easy to get customers to listen to them. I understand everyone's frustration when others are not listening. However, if one believes in the concept of karma, shouldn't he or she take ownership of his or her communication instead of trying to blame the ineffectiveness on the other person? There is no law of good karma regarding communication that states, "The more you complain about the ineffectiveness of your communication, the more likely it is that you will get rewarded with successful communication." Instead, in both the personal and the business world, successful communication starts with one person trying to understand the other person, clearly identifying what he or

she wants to communicate, and then putting forth his or her best effort to communicate. Only then is it likely that the individual will be rewarded with good communication back. Here are some parts of communication that I feel are important.

- **The Right Amount of Communication Matters:** The right amount of communication is essential for success. Balance in communication is important to achieve, as too much communication can be overwhelming, and too little might not be enough to form a full impression.
- **Using Headlines and Taglines:** Often, brands use headlines and taglines randomly, thinking about what they want to be associated with. Instead, brands must consider how customers should see them, as that is the true reality of a brand.
- **A Common Language:** Speaking the language of the customer is essential, as it is not fair to expect the customer to learn the language of the brand to make purchases.
- **Bread-Crumbing**: This is a great way of respecting the customer's intelligence and creating a bond with the customer.
- **Science of Communication:** After reviewing all the communication elements, it is important to review the science of communication to get a clear idea of why communications fail.

Don't Start as a Fire Hydrant

Imagine your date is thirsty. She wants a glass of water, and you oblige her by acting as a fire hydrant and drowning her in an overflow of water. That is bound not to go down as a kind gesture.

Let me go back to a simple dating situation. You are going out on a first date. You want to be prepared. You might read books or ask friends about what to wear, say, and do on the first date. Walking in wearing a glittering multicolored shirt, starting the date with a long description of yourself, talking a lot without listening, pushing too hard for a second date, or following a how-to-close-a-date-successfully rule that you downloaded from the Internet will likely not give the first impression you want.

If you did those things, do you know what you just did? You communicated successfully to your date that you are too much into yourself, and you cannot blame her if she decides she does not want to go out with you on a second date. What could you have done differently? You could have paused and taken the Am I? test. Ask yourself these questions:

- Am I coming across as too self-centered?
- Am I being unbearable?
- Am I not being sincere?
- Am I not proud of the way I am coming across?

If the answer to any of the questions is yes, then you know there will be no good dating karma for you. In the same way, there can be communication pitfalls in the business world too when a brand overcommunicates.

Client Pitch for a Tech Brand

Let me use the example of a new technology brand that is trying to create a client pitch. They start with big tech words that are not used in everyday language and then use them in a paragraph (not a sentence) to describe what they stand for. When they do this, I feel they are asking the customer to take a comprehension test. They are effectively asking the customer, "Can you read the entire paragraph and figure out what we stand for? Can you?"

Customers have lives, and they don't have the time or inclination to play games.

I am referring to situations in which a brand says too many things but nothing that connects to the customer. To showcase that, here is a simple test I want you to take the next time you are driving down a freeway. Look at any billboard that you pass. What did the billboard communicate? A lot of things maybe. An average person driving at sixty-five miles an hour only gets a few seconds to read a billboard. Now ask yourself the following: Was the billboard designed for you to get the message in a few seconds, or was it so cluttered that you did not even get who the advertiser was?

This urge to say too many things or everything about a brand is a common trait with some brands. To communicate effectively, a brand must identify things about the brand that current customers need to know to be assured they made the right choice and that future customers need to know to choose a brand. To arrive at the brand message, discover and articulately define the following:

- What was the customer expecting when he or she walked in today?
- What does the customer want to walk away with?
- Why does the customer care about our existence?
- What is the heart of the brand that we want to share with the customer?

Once you have answers to these questions, answers that only your brand can own, it is important for the brand to communicate in its way, being sincere and authentic. This is similar to the dating example, in which the man paused before he started sharing everything about himself and gave his date an opportunity to get to know the real him. In the same way, the brand can communicate proactively key information about it. The brand makes the rest of the information available to the customer to discover at his or her own pace. There is no need to overwhelm the customer with everything about the brand.

Random Taglines

As a brand stays away from overcommunicating, sometimes communicating in just a few words might not necessarily result in effective communication. The other side of communication, saying too few words, is just as bad as saying too many. This section will show two main areas of communication: taglines and memos. Think about the first date. If you choose not to share anything significant about you, your date might think you are not interested in him or her. Hence, striking the right balance is the key, and the right balance depends on the two people and their current state.

An area where most brands communicate in a crisp manner is the tagline. Unlike the logo, which is nearly permanent, taglines or descriptors can be changed over time as a brand evolves. But if a brand can come up with a tagline that can stand the test of time, it defines the brand. Taglines are a way for brands to define themselves in the customers' minds. This is an area where personal relationships and customer relationships are different. In a personal relationship, where there is a one-to-one relationship, there is no need for a short description. The only place you might need a descriptor is in the title of your online profile. Any use of it beyond that can come across as annoying. A man named Dan cannot introduce himself to his date as Dan the Man. It would come across as superficial. That said, there was one instance I experienced in which I was impressed by a friend of mine when he introduced himself using a tagline. His name is Rod Fudge, and he always introduced himself as "Rod Fudge. Fudge just like the candy—yummy." The reason it worked for Rod was because of his authenticity and his comfort in using the self-descriptor or human tagline.

Even though taglines don't work in personal relationships, Rod Fudge's example always reminded me that a brand needs to be comfortable with its tagline, and the tagline should connect to the brand's promise. I learned that a tagline is not always a literal description of a brand's offering; instead, it is a brand's chant or slogan. It works in conjunction with the logo. During my corporate days, two of the brands I worked with found new taglines. In both cases, the taglines have stood the test of time. Let me share a little more about them.

- "Better Ingredients. Better Pizza": This was a classic case of Papa John's, a national pizza brand, stating with pride that it offers better pizza than its competition. But in the world of puffery, where every brand is claiming to be the best, it was not easy to make the claim and own it. The pizza brand shared its DNA of better ingredients so that it could own that perception in the customer's mind. The reason I say that the phrase "better ingredients" is the DNA of the brand is because that was the value by which the founder lived every day, which made it the brand's true definer. It was not a case of a brand simply making a claim; instead, it was a brand committing till the end of time to invest in getting better.
- "Eat, Drink, Play": This was the tagline of Jillian's Entertainment, which had huge entertainment properties featuring multiple restaurants, bowling alleys, gaming areas, and night clubs. In this case, the power of the three words defined the tagline. Similar to the Papa John's example, the word *play* defined the highest level of the end benefit that the brand stood for, and *eat* and *drink* were brand descriptors. Also, "Eat, Drink, Play" made customers feel empowered to be who they wanted to be at Jillian's.

Not only have both these taglines stood the test of time, but also, you will see numerous instances of similar taglines in different industries. I believe imitation is the highest form of flattery and proof of leadership. Each tagline, just like Rod Fudge's, connected to its brand's authentic promise. If you put one of these taglines under any of its competitions' logos, it would not fit.

Most Effective Press Release Ever?

Short, crisp communications can be effective in the business world too, but only if they are planned to perfection. One of my favorite communications of all times is the 1995 press release by Michael Jordan. On March 18, 1995, Michael Jordan came out of retirement and issued a simple two-word press release: "I'm back!" That was all he needed to say. Michael did not explain why he was coming back or what his goals were. Instead, he simply shared the news of his return to basketball fans and created excitement about his return. Every sports media headline included those two words from Michael, and the message was successfully communicated to all sports fans around the globe.

Speak a Common Language

A brand must understand the secret of communication to be successful. If I send you an e-mail and you feel in reading it that I have shared something with only you and that what I have shared is relevant only in the present, then you are more likely to pay attention to it. One has to identify the right communication strategy to be successful. Sometimes brands define their customer service experience rigidly and force employees to follow the steps literally.

Here are some examples.

Forced to Listen to Today's Specials

At a sit-down restaurant, the server comes to the table and recites the entire list of meat-centric specials only to find out that guests are vegetarian, so none of the specials are relevant to them. Specials are exciting news in any restaurant, but why will a customer be excited about menu items that are outside his or her chosen diet?

Software Terms of Agreement

When you are installing new software, you are forced to read and accept pages of contract agreement terms. Come on—who reads all the details in the contract documents? I understand that the software companies need to protect themselves, but isn't the chance of the customer following the contract higher if the customer knows exactly what is in the contract? Why can't the software company simplify its contract to a simple format? For example, how about the following?

- You can only use the license on one machine.
- You will not copy the software.
- You will not give the software to others.
- The company owns the software.

There might be more contract elements, but I truly believe that the customer is more likely to follow the contract conditions if he or she is made aware of the contract.

Safety Announcement in a Flight

Before a flight takes off, based on FAA regulations, every passenger is required to be made aware of the safety procedures. If you are flying, either you will see a safety video appear on the screen, or you will witness a mechanical, sometimes rushed, mime show by the flight attendants with a background narration. I agree that awareness of safety procedures is important, as in the event of an emergency, those procedures could save lives. If that is the case, shouldn't airlines be creative in successfully communicating the safety regulations to the passengers instead of just checking the box marked "Safety demonstration performed"?

In each of the cases above, the brand chose to communicate in the legal language and not take into account that customers do not speak that way. They also forced team members to speak that language. Brands need to understand that they have a lot of flexibility in how they communicate, and to communicate effectively, brands should embrace the communication language used by customers. The tone of a brand's communication with its customers is set by its internal communication and processes. Here are some examples of breakthrough internal communication that define the communication culture in an organization.

Training Using a Video Game

One of the first breakthrough training programs I witnessed was in the late 1990s at a restaurant company. The company developed a video game titled

What Is Wrong with the Picture? In different versions of the game, there would be elements that were intentionally incorrect. A team member was asked to identify each of the wrong things in the shortest time available. Examples of what was wrong included an empty napkin holder, an empty beverage cup on the counter, overflowing trash, dirty floors, and more. Team members looked at this as a competitive game, and scoring the lowest time became a bragging right in the company. What was amazing was that in the process of playing these video games, team members unconsciously became aware of noticing things that needed attention in the restaurants and were conditioned on how to fix things.

Lessons from a Comic Book

A retail brand came out with another unique training tool. They put the training content in a comic book format. The characters in the comic book were the brand's founder and team members. These were short comic stories that targeted different aspects of training.

Speaking in Everyday Language

A brand realized that it had written all its employee manuals in the legal language. No one reads a manual written in legal language unless one is forced to read it. To change this, the brand rewrote every manual using everyday language, and that made it easy for employees to read the manuals.

In each case, the training departments realized that the target audience for the information was the younger generation, and a traditional training session lecture did not have high traction with them. Hence, a format like a video game or a comic book made the information interesting and familiar for the target audience. In both cases, the tools caused high levels of interest among the target audience, and creating interest among the target audience gave the training tool a big jump start. The team members easily absorbed the content and learned better and faster, as they were not thinking that they were learning. Breakthrough success came from identifying ways to communicate training content most effectively to the customers.

Overall, communication seems like a complicated topic, as only a few brands have broken the mold and started communicating in simple everyday language. But shouldn't that be the norm of communication? If a rocket scientist were dating a psychologist, shouldn't each make an effort to communicate in a language that is simple and understandable to the other? If the rocket scientist chose to communicate her feelings using mathematical formulas and the psychologist started communicating his feelings using Freudian principles, it would be quite confusing. The onus of successful communication is on the one communicating; hence, making the information comprehensible to the other person is essential for success.

Bread-Crumbing Communication

Thus far, I have talked about brands sharing everything about themselves with customers and overwhelming them, communicating just a few words and not getting through, and using legal jargon that customers choose to ignore immediately. The sweet spot in which communication is most effective is a perfect medium. Let me share with you another dimension: the bread-crumb theory. I found a great example of this in the movie *Be Cool*. In the movie, the character of Chili Palmer, played by John Travolta, has a famous one-liner that he says over and over: "I will tell you what you need to know, maybe less." It might be the way John Travolta delivers the line, or it might be the context of the story in which the line is used, but either way, the line made a big impact on me. I have used this line to demonstrate the issue to my clients quite a few times, especially in PR communication, in which giving the right amount of information is very important.

This part of communication is a personal favorite topic of mine, as it is based on the following concept: "The customer is smart and deserves respect for his or her intelligence." By respecting the customer's intelligence, the brand also comes across as intelligent and connects with the customer on a deeper level. Here is one of the best examples of doing it right that I can share with you.

One of the leading fast-casual Mexican restaurants has perfected this art of communication in its billboards.

- "Empty—Full": This billboard says only two words: *empty* and *full*. Below the word *empty* is a picture of a burrito in foil, and below the word *full* is an empty, crumpled piece of foil. When I saw the billboard for the first time, I got it: "After I eat the burrito, I will be full. Also, the burrito is so good that I will eat the entire burrito."

Once I got it, I felt that others might not get it, and that made me feel a deeper connection with the brand. The brand made me feel smart.

- "420ish": As I used to drive to the University of Colorado to teach marketing classes, I would see billboards of the same brand with only one word—*420ish*—and the picture of the burrito in foil. I have to admit that I drove past that billboard quite a few times and never got it. Once, I asked my students what the billboard stood for, and one of my students laughed and told me, "Professor Sen, it is good that you do not get it. It is not for you to get." The rest of the students giggled, and I sensed that the students felt an exclusive connection with the brand because they got the message, while their professor did not get it.

- "Prasadam": As that same brand went to the northeast, where a large vegetarian Hindu population exists, the brand wanted to identify a way of communicating with the group that the food at the restaurant can be "vegetarian vegetarian," meaning no nonvegetarian contamination. They must have studied every aspect of the Hindu lifestyle, and they came up with a billboard that said, "Prasadam," with the picture of the burrito in foil below it. Many of you might not get the significance of this, but I have to share with you that I got this one. When a Hindu goes to the temple, after paying respect to all the gods, he then eats the blessed food, which is called *prasadam*. No nonvegetarian food item ever enters the temple; hence, prasadam is the purest and most assured form of vegetarian food for a Hindu. Thus, the billboard did its job. I am sure that Hindu customers must have felt special seeing that the brand cared about them by talking to them in a language only they understand. That must have made them feel the same way my students at the University of Colorado at Boulder felt when they got the "420ish" billboard and I did not get it.

The bread-crumb theory guides the customer through a journey of discovering for him- or herself the brand's message. Making customers feel smart and respected for their intelligence connects them better to the brand. There is also an element of feeling special in this, as the brand selectively communicates with different customers. This is similar to speaking in simple codes that allow for exclusive communication between two people. When my daughter was young, we created a code in which we referred to people by spelling their names backward. Hence, Raka Sen became Akar Nes, and I became Nurja. This speaking in codes added excitement to our father-daughter communication and made us feel special. As others around us did not immediately get it, our code made us feel smart. Hence, communication that is exclusive and recognizes the intelligence of the customer can go a long way in defining a brand's relationship with its customers.

The Science of Communication

In any relationship, communication is one of the biggest drivers of success. Brands must learn how to communicate successfully internally and also with the customer. Within a company, different departments can work together successfully only if they effectively communicate. Failure to communicate can weaken even the best teams.

I want to emphasize that better communication is more than copying each other in e-mails or participating in the other department's staff meetings. That, to me, is transparency, and often, too much transparency is confusing. I feel communication is more science than art. The art of communication comes to one naturally. Hence, let me focus on the science that is behind effective communication. As you go through this section, you will see that there are different kinds of communication blunders: failure to communicate, miscommunication, and total lack of communication. Understanding the purpose of your communication is critical to being successful and effective as a brand. In this case, the finish line is effective communication.

Here is a simple everyday communication example. I will use this to discuss different concepts.

> Person A: "I just landed at the airport. The flight was bumpy, and quite a few people on the flight were falling sick. I think I am ready to be picked up."
> Person B: "Glad you are here. It is raining quite hard. See you soon."

Let me translate this into a simple communication-effectiveness module.

The Simple Communication Module

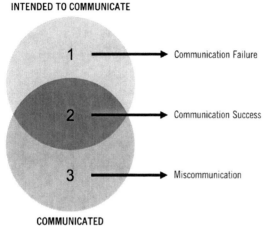

Figure 1.

In figure 1, the top circle is what one intended to communicate, and the bottom circle is what was actually communicated, or what the audience understood. In any communication, there is never a 100 percent overlap; hence, three different areas arise.

Area 1: Communication Failure
In this area, one wanted to communicate a thought or idea, but the target audience did not get it. The smaller this area is, the more effective you were. In our example, the communication failures happened when person A failed to communicate where to pick her up (e.g., Terminal 1, arrival door 403), and person B failed to communicate that he was only five minutes away. You might feel surprised by the sudden appearance of graphs and Venn diagrams in the book and might be asking yourself where they came from. I felt that the graphs and Venn diagrams were needed to demonstrate the art of the science that drives successful communication. Getting better at communication is beyond a few simple tactics.

Area 2: Communication Success
This area marks successful communication. The larger this area is, the more effective you were. In our example, person A successfully communicated that she has landed and is ready to be picked up. Person B successfully communicated that he is on the way and close to reaching the airport.

Area 3: Miscommunication
This area is the most worrisome area. These are thoughts and ideas that one communicated but did not intend to communicate. When this

miscommunication happens, the audience walks away with a message different from the desired message. The reason this area is the most worrisome is that one has no clue what these messages are, and they are the messages with which the target audience will define the brand. Consider a presentation in which any time there was a question, you answered it by saying, "Let me think," and then you proceeded to look at your notes, search back and forth through your pages, and then answer the question. This type of indecision might make the attendees unsure of your expert status, and once doubt creeps in, they might start questioning every aspect of the presentation. A better example yet might be to think of a couple about to celebrate a wedding anniversary. While visiting the mall, the couple pauses in front of a jewelry store and looks at an expensive necklace before moving on to other stores. In this process, the husband might have set an expectation in his wife's mind that she is getting that necklace for their upcoming anniversary.

In the original communication we looked at, the following is what happened: person A needed to communicate that she had landed and was ready to be picked up. It would have helped person B to know when and where person A needed to be picked up. Person B, in turn, needed to get the pickup information and needed to say that he was only five minutes away. When person A talked about the bumpy flight and the passengers getting sick, person B might have taken away from this that person A is not feeling well. He might even think of canceling the dinner reservation he made for them. Because person B said that it was raining hard, person A might think that person B could be running a little late. As you can see, connecting back to the diagram, it is important to know what you want to communicate and stick to it with the discipline to be successful.

Most miscommunication comes from two sources.

1. Expressions and Gestures: Here are a few examples of expressions and gestures that commonly cause miscommunication.

- Looking at the clock too often might indicate that you are in a rush to get somewhere else.
- Answering texts during a conversation might be perceived as lack of interest in the conversation.
- On a Skype call, if you cannot hear the person clearly, you might move close to the laptop screen and squint to try to hear better. The person on the other side might feel that that you are irritated or annoyed because of the gestures.

2. Leaving Open Issues: You might add a graph to illustrate a side comment in a presentation, but unless you connect it 100 percent to your presentation, you are bound to feed your intelligent target audience with distracting information that will lead to miscommunication. Everything you communicate must have a purpose. In our example, miscommunication happened when person A talked about the bumpy flight and passengers getting sick, and person B mentioned that it was raining hard.

It makes sense to me that successful communication results are a blend of art and science, because customers make decisions both emotionally and rationally. The art and the science together can make an impact. Successful communication is an ongoing journey and needs constant feedback and review to improve. To build a lifelong relationship with your customer, it is important to consider the communication strategies you are using that are helping or hindering that relationship's success.

Michael Jordan vs. Tiger Woods

Now let me go back to the example of Michael Jordan's communication in his simple two-word press release: "I'm back!" It was so effective because it identified the only thing the world needed to know, and that is what the communication focused on. There was nothing else that we needed to know.

On the other hand, on November 30, 2009, when Tiger Woods lost control of his SUV outside his Florida mansion, the world only wanted to know two things:

...ld Tiger be okay?
...uld he be able to play golf again soon?

But...d of proactively focusing on communicating these two elements, Tiger Woods's team let the media dictate the communication. As a result, people started searching for information, and the media flooded them with noise. Here are some of the bits of noise that came out in the first few days after the accident:

- Woods pulled out of his driveway at 2:25 a.m.
- His vehicle hit a fire hydrant and a tree in his neighbor's yard.
- His wife used a golf club to smash out the back window to help get him out.
- He was mumbling after the accident.
- He had been taking prescription pain medication for an injury, which could explain why he seemed somewhat out of it at the scene.

If you only put these noise elements together, it becomes a story of a man who took pain medication and tried to drive his car in the middle of the night. He was so out of it that he could not even get out of the driveway, as he hit a fire hydrant and a tree in his neighbor's yard. The accident must have been serious, as his wife had to use a golf club to smash out the back window to help get him out.

These noise elements took the story away from what we needed to know and made it a tabloid story that had nothing to do with golf, other than that a golf club was used for the wrong reason (i.e., to break the back window and not to hit a ball on a golf course).

A review of both stories shows the power of perfect communication, in which perfection is defined by both content and timing.

Karma of Giving

As I was trying to build the global alumni network for a university, I was appalled by the level of existing frustrations: "The alumni group does not help me with jobs," "The alumni group does not connect me with mentors who can move my career to the next level," and "The alumni group doesn't bring us value-added offerings, such as discounted services." The list goes on and on.

As I was getting overwhelmed by the complaints about lack of giving, I started asking questions of mine: "What is this alumni group anyway? Isn't each one of you a piece that builds this group? What is the one thing that you can give to the group? If each of you gives something that other group members can use, don't you think there will be something for everyone to get from the group? And don't you think that once you give from your heart, it is more likely that others will reward you by giving back?" In the business world, giving is often mistaken as bait, like that used in fishing; it is a way to get customers to come to a business. True giving in the business world should be inspired by the concept of good karma.

There are four parts of giving that are important to focus on.

1. **What:** What you give matters. Brands often give things to guests that are convenient for them to give. Instead, they should look from the point of view of the customers to identify what they think of the gifts.
2. **When:** When you give matters. This has been an eye-opener for me, as even the best gift coming at the wrong time might not be appreciated to its true potential.
3. **Taking Back Giving**: When you stop giving something that you were offering on an ongoing basis, it can be tricky. Instead of the customer appreciating the giving all the previous times, he or she might choose to focus on the absence of the gift and say, "Why are you not giving that to me anymore?"
4. **Thanking from the Heart:** Finally, how should you respond when someone shows appreciation? This is an interesting area that a lot of brands miss. When a customer is really touched by a brand and initiates a contact, a sincere, authentic response from the brand moves the relationship forward.

In each of the four areas, keeping the recipient in mind and focusing on his or her need is essential for building a long-term relationship.

When a Grandma Called Me Stupid

What you give matters. First, let me talk about gifts that are convenient to give. Here is an example from my personal life.

She Was Not into Photography

Within a year of getting married, I was trying to find the most amazing gift for my then wife. I searched long and hard and then found an Olympus camera. In those days, I was a graduate student who did not have a camera and wanted one. However, the budget was tight for a newly married couple going to graduate school, so I decided to get an Olympus camera for my then wife for her first birthday after our marriage.

When I gave her the gift, all neatly wrapped, I was excited. When she opened it, my excitement overshadowed her polite yet surprised look. I had the biggest smile on my face, and I said, "Yes?" I was waiting for her excitement. I did not get it.

But did I care? I did not. I was happy that I'd gotten her what I had wanted to get her and what had been convenient to give her. Today, when I look back, I am amazed at how caught up in the moment I was, looking at life from my perspective and not even thinking that another perspective could exist. I gave her what I wanted myself and not what she wanted. Years have passed, and she and I are divorced, but I still feel some degree of embarrassment when I think of that gift. Over the years, that embarrassment has educated me on being sensitive to the needs of those around me, especially when I am giving a gift or reward. That lesson has been the cornerstone of all the work I have done in the field of loyalty.

When a Customer Did Not Want to Pay a Lower Price

On the business side, the situation was similar. I was working for a national pizza company. With my experience in the field, I was confident that no one knew pizza marketing better than I did. As you might be guessing, any time anyone in the business world thinks that he or she knows more than everyone else, that person is in for a rude awakening. I wanted to run some ideas by customers and decided to do a series of focus groups with loyal customers.

With one of these focus groups, I presented a successful idea that had worked in the company: "You buy ten pizzas, and after that, you can buy pizzas for the rest of the year at a special price of seven dollars." Now, to put things into perspective, in those days, a large pizza was valued at ten dollars, so this was akin to an offer of 30 percent off without any coupons. Also, I had followed the cardinal rule of loyalty programs, as this offer was the best deal the customer could get from the pizza company.

During the focus group, I was my usual self. I was romancing the customers, making them feel excited by being there and getting their feedback. It was evident that this idea was working, as nearly every customer was buying more pizzas from my company and was not thinking of going anywhere else. Isn't that the ideal goal of a loyalty program?

But there was something missing. I got the answer when, toward the end of one of the focus groups, I said to the respondents, "What else can we do to make sure that you never buy pizzas from anyone else? Think without any constraints or restrictions. Do not hold back!"

An older woman in the group wanted to educate me and said, "Son, looks like you are not that smart. In fact, you may be a little slow to get things. I hate to call you stupid."

I had no clue where she was going, but she was not one to stop because I was confused. She went on to say, "Look, son, not once, not twice, and not just five times but ten times"—she showed her ten fingers as she said this—"I have shown you that I can afford to buy your large pizzas for ten dollars. I have problems with the price. Do not get me wrong; I like the fact that you reduced the price to seven dollars, but you know what it made me realize? It made me realize that earlier, you were really hosing me at ten dollars. Even now, you are making a lot of money at seven dollars. So the deal made me question everything about your restaurant."

Wow, that was some insight. My reducing the price and offering a sweet deal made people like her doubt my brand and, in fact, weakened the connection between her and my restaurant. That meant I had given up profits for my brand to fall in her eyes. After the price drop, she was visiting more often, as she felt addicted to the seven-dollar price point, but the connection was not strong enough to survive if I could not offer that seven-dollar price point in the future.

I paused and then looked at her and asked, "What one thing can I do for you that will make you come to me every time you order a pizza?"

She was ready with her response. "Treat me special. Find out about me. Give me things that I want. Give me things that you do not give everyone else."

"And what might that be?" I asked.

She gave me a look that seemed to say, "Wait, and be patient. I am telling you." She went on to say, "If I am truly so special, why not put my pizza at the front of the line every time I order? Put me and the rest of the people in the group first."

Wow. How could I have missed that? I thought.

I have experienced this every time I have flown. Even on a delayed flight, the preferred fliers get to board first, effectively saying, "Na-na boo-boo, you cannot have this," to the rest of the customers. Yes, being special means getting things that not everyone gets.

Now, I started this story by saying that there was something missing in my loyalty program. Before this eye-opening experience, I was sure that my marketing team had the best loyalty idea with the discounted pizza deal. I'd always thought the operators were not behind it, and they were the reason this idea had not reached its true potential.

However, this conversation made me realize that what was missing was the brand's heart. The brand had selected an idea that was easy to track and implement, and in some ways, since it was topped with a deal that was so incredible, the result, measured by sales increase, was bound to happen. But in the process, the brand's connection with the customer was not getting any stronger, and customers perceived the brand to be a seven-dollar pizza brand instead of a ten-dollar pizza brand. As a result, the relationship with the customer became impersonal and merely transactional, though the seven-dollar price would make it difficult for the customer to leave the brand.

Next time you are trying to reward your customers, ask the following questions:

1. Is it a true gift or a bribe?
2. Are you giving what is easy or convenient for you to give?
3. Will the customer appreciate the gift?
4. Are you excited all the way from your heart to give the gift?
5. When you meet a grandma who got the gift, will she call you stupid for not understanding her needs and for giving her the gift?

A Dating Loyalty Card

I wish I had translated this business example into a dating example earlier, as I would have immediately seen the problem. This way of trying to hold on to loyal customers would translate into a dating loyalty card in which you made the following promises to your date:

- After five dates, you get a dozen carnations.
- After ten dates, you get a dozen roses.
- After fifteen dates, you get a box of chocolates.

If anyone was silly enough to implement this, he should have asked himself if his date was going out with him for carnations, roses, or chocolates. By putting this program in place, did he trivialize himself? I believe in celebrating every milestone, and it can be cute to celebrate dating milestones, but the celebration of life has to be spontaneous and not based on a loyalty card idea.

If this idea of a loyalty program is silly in a romantic relationship, why is it so popular in the business world? These are some reasons brands jump into implementing a loyalty program:

- It is easy to implement.
- It is measurable. The brand can measure the effectiveness of the program and compare the effectiveness of different offers used in the loyalty program.
- The brand feels it has some control over the customer and feels that it is influencing the customer's decision.

But here is what brands miss. Unless the brand is a value brand, which is a category price leader, the brand might be training the customer not to visit the brand more often but to buy smarter. The loyalty program is training the customer to buy because of the program incentives and not because the product is perceived to be a clearly better option.

Now think about this: If you are a competitive brand coming into the market, what should you do? You might study the loyalty program used by the leading brand and then use the incentives from the program more aggressively to generate trial among competitive customers. However, if the brand built a long-term relationship with the customers, then it would be difficult for you to generate any trial among their customers.

A Free Bra on My Birthday

As I said, what you give matters. Now let me talk about gifts that can break a relationship. When you are in a romantic relationship, if you give random gifts or inappropriate gifts, they can be relationship killers.

Now that you know what kind of gifts to give, should you consider automating gift giving in your relationship? Businesses automate customer rewards just as one sets up a recurring meeting based on a criterion. In the world of databases, I believe every brand I have ever interacted with as a customer collected all available information on me. I feel as if each brand has a secret file of information on me. Sometimes brands share information or augment their databases with my credit card spending. On top of that, my browser history and my smartphone travel details are all stored. In short, it seems most brands know more about me than I know about me.

Any brand I frequently use has a lot of information on me, and one of those data points is my date of birth. It is somewhat uncomfortable or worrisome when different brands start sending me semipersonal wishes on my birthday. All birthday wishes are nearly the same. Each has a mostly impersonal message wishing me a happy birthday and also includes an offer encouraging me to visit the brand.

One year, I decided to review all the birthday wishes different brands had sent me. I received a few from restaurants, one from a regional transportation company, and one from a lingerie company.

A Free Burrito That Wasn't Actually Free

I know you are intrigued by my relationship with the lingerie company, but let me start with the restaurants first. One of them offered me a buy-one-and-get-one-free burrito deal. I thought for a while and realized that on my birthday, if I found a friend who would come with me and pay for his burrito, I would then get a free burrito. Now, how would I find that friend for this adventure, as most of my friends would love to pay for my food on my birthday? Even if we went out on my birthday, would it not be awkward for me to tell my friend that I was choosing the restaurant because they'd sent me an offer and that my meal would be paid for when he paid for his? I do not know about you, but for me, that offer had the word *awkward* written all over it, so that offer made it to the recycling bin.

Expect Me to Drive Five Miles for a Free Cookie?

The other two restaurant offers were for free desserts. One was from a fast-casual restaurant that offered me a free birthday cookie. There was no purchase necessary. I felt good about that offer. I liked the fact that I was not forced to buy anything. But think for a second. Would I just stop by to get my free cookie? Or was the restaurant betting that if I showed up to collect my free cookie, I would buy something else? That made me feel that the gift was not a gift from the heart. Now, if the restaurant had made the offer non-date-specific, I might have used it. Similarly, when my golf buddy gives me a golf polo, he does not say that I can only wear it on my birthday. I wear it when I want to. In the same way, my free cookie, if it were truly mine, would be there for me anytime I wanted to go get it.

When I (Nearly) Refused Free Dessert

The other restaurant offering free dessert was an Italian restaurant. They made an offer that I could not refuse. They offered me the free dessert anytime during the month of my birthday. They even printed my name on the offer. I was excited, as I could see myself visiting the restaurant. A few days after my birthday, I decided to go to the restaurant for dinner. I ordered a salad and meticulously finished every piece of lettuce, as I wanted to get to my reward. I wanted my free dessert. Finally, I ordered it, and when the time came to pay, I showed my gift certificate. I was expecting my server to smile and spontaneously wish me a happy birthday. I was hoping that she and her coworkers would not show up at my table and start singing.

But what happened next was unexpected. The server, instead of wishing me a happy birthday, examined the coupon carefully. I started to feel uncomfortable and told her that it was valid for the month of June, and she smiled and said that she'd noticed that already. Then she said that the coupon was not transferable and was for my use only. Hence, she wanted to check my driver's license. I thought that was an odd request; none of my friends had ever asked for my driver's license before they wished me happy birthday or gave me a gift. I felt that she was simply doing her job and following company protocol, so I obliged and gave her my driver's license. Then I was sure that the warm and fuzzy reaction from her would finally come. I thought that she would just glance at my driver's license and say something funny, such as "You do not look any older than twenty-five." But that did not happen. She said that I could not use the coupon, as the name printed on the coupon was Senarjun, with no last name. I tried to explain to her that Senarjun was my last name and first name juxtaposed and printed without any space. I could not believe that I was in such a pathetic situation, pleading for my free dessert, but I was too far into the game to just give up. Then she took the game away from me, as she decided to talk to her supervisor. She took my driver's license and my coupon and went to see her boss, the manager. By now, I did not want the free dessert. I was ready to pay and leave. The manager returned with the server, and they gave my driver's license back to me. Then the manager explained that they could only give the free dessert to the person whose name was on the coupon, and that person could use the coupon only once. He also explained that there was a lot of misuse of coupons, and because of that, they had started this policy. I was confused, as I did not know why the manager was telling me all this. As he went on explaining the policy, this is what I started hearing: "I know you were trying to misuse the coupon and steal a free dessert from us. I am giving you time and explaining the rules so that you can confess on your own. That way, we can close this issue and move forward." I was tired of hearing the same thing rehashed differently by the manager, who was making no effort to resolve the situation.

All of a sudden, the manager paused and decided to do something managerial. He looked at the server and said, "For this instance, comp the dessert. Put the manager's discount on it as you ring it up. When you ring it, wait for me to come authorize it. I am proud of the way you followed the restaurant's policy and helped me resolve the issue. But make sure he uses the dessert today, as I cannot allow him to come back another day for the dessert." For those not familiar with the term, *comp* meant making the item free, or complimentary, at the discretion of the manager. The manager instructed the server while ignoring my presence, as he did not think about what I would feel as I heard his words. I did not want the manager's charity. Now the issue was no longer about my free dessert. I was humiliated and upset. I had wasted too much time on getting this resolved. I never wanted to get a free dessert this way. When I finally left the restaurant, I realized that neither the server nor the manager had wished me a happy birthday. I am okay if a friend of mine forgets my birthday, as I am forgetful myself. But if a friend invited me out on my birthday and then did not wish me a happy birthday, to me, that would be hurtful. So no need to say this was bad karma from the Italian restaurant.

Free Ride on My Birthday

The next birthday offer I received was from a regional transportation company. They sent me a simple letter wishing me happy birthday and offering me four free days of travel. By now, I was suspicious of any birthday offers and wanted to read all the fine print. I was surprised to find that the offer had no fine print, and it did not say that only I could use them. The offers did not have any expiration date on them either. I gave them to my daughter, and she used the passes for rides to downtown. *Wow,* I thought. The company had given me something truly free that I could find a use for on my terms. Now, that is a true gift, and their genuineness touched me. Finally, some good karma came my way on my birthday.

No Bra for Me

Now I'll tell you about the gift I was saving for last, which you were waiting for patiently, the most startling one. It was from a lingerie company. Before you roll your eyes, I have to assure you that I had no idea why a lingerie company wished me happy birthday and offered me a free bra. Yes, they offered me a free bra with no strings attached. A lot of thoughts came to my mind. I even thought that one of my funny golf buddies had set me up. Although I was lost and somewhat shocked and embarrassed, I finally figured out how this happened. I had been to their store a few times with my teenage daughter. Of course, the only reason I was in the store was so that I could let my daughter pay using my credit card. It was uncomfortable for me, the dad, to be in the store with my teenage daughter. On top of it, when we were checking out, my daughter told me that she would get a price discount if we filled out a form. At that point in time, I was ready to do anything to get out of that place, so I completed the form, and duh—I got rewarded with a free bra on my birthday. I have to clarify for those of you who are wondering: I did not use the coupon. Just getting the coupon was embarrassment enough.

Now, what happened in these examples? In each case, some high-energy marketing person wanted to implement a birthday program. As the marketing team developed the program, they felt that success of the program was measured by the number of customers' birthdays they collected. They determined what offer to give and measured what percentage of offers were redeemed. They must have put a lot of effort into collecting names, birthdays, and contact information. Then came the time to select the offer. Based on my experience regarding how similar decisions were made, I would bet that the marketing person wanted to find an offer whereby the brand would not be losing money by giving away product or would at least break even. This kind of financial-analysis-driven offer helps show the upside of the offer with little risk, as the promotion would result in incremental sales and would not cost the stores anything. But they missed one fact. Giving me a truly free gift on my birthday would have resulted in my becoming a fan of the brand and patronizing it more often. Even with the most complicated math, one or two extra visits from me would have made the offer worthwhile.

In the Italian restaurant example, the marketing team was keen to make sure that the coupons were not misused; hence, they put a strict operations protocol in place that store team members needed to follow. So even though I was thoroughly irate with the server and the manager, the operations protocol prevented them from doing anything meaningful to make me happy. If marketing implements a program but the employees' hands are tied in following protocol, it requires a truly maverick operations team member to cross the line and do what it takes to wow the guest.

Finally, I want to address the lingerie company's gift. They had a great promotion that gave customers an incentive to give their names, dates of birth, and other contact information. However, shouldn't they have separated the buyer and the user of the product from the payer? I am sure I am not the only dad who went to the store with his daughter and paid with his credit card. Therefore, sending an offer that embarrassed me just because my name was in the database was a case of using the database without thinking. In this case, the operations team members were all doing their best to encourage customers to give their contact information, but marketing did not qualify the database. Hence, the hard work done by store-level team members resulted in dads like me receiving offers for free bras. The result was not good karma in any sense.

After all that adventure, I am sure I will no longer open any more birthday offers from anyone. As you look at my gift adventure, it becomes evident that good customer karma does not come from automated responses; instead, it comes when a business is sincere and touches my heart. I would even go so far as to say it is better not to give an automated gift and make the customer say, "Whoa," if a business cannot think of a meaningful gift from the heart that makes the customer say, "Wow." The best gifts are ones that make the customer feel that the gift was given only to him or her. That makes it a special experience that will get the customer to say, "Wow."

Based on the above examples, here are a few questions you should ask yourself before you start building a reward program.

1. Who will be the primary beneficiary of the reward program? If the answer to this question is not the customer, then you should not go forward with a reward program.
2. What kind of a relationship does the customer want to have? If customers want to connect with your brand once a year, I do not think they want a relationship in which you contact them on their birthdays to offer them coupons. If the relationship evolves to a point where you have earned the right to communicate with a customer on his or her birthday, please make sure that the gift or gesture from you connects with the customer and that you are not giving what seems like a good gift to you.

Effectively, what I am trying to get to is this: please do not give a free bra coupon to a single dad.

No More Warm Nuts for Me

Consider this scenario. The first few dates went great, and you start thinking about how to be more efficient. The first few times, you picked her up for the date and dropped her off at her home after the date. You even opened the car door for her. After every date and the morning after, you sent her cute texts. On the third date, you decide to make things easier for you. At the end of the date, instead of taking her home, you arrange for a cab to take her home. On the next date, you do not pick her up, and soon you stop the postdate texts. In the beginning, there were things you were doing consistently that touched your date's heart. Your actions were simple, classy gestures, and she appreciated them. Then, one day, these stopped. You stopped getting out of the car and opening the car door for her. You stopped texting her after she got home, and over time, the day-after texts too started to be absent. Your date might perceive the tapering off or withdrawal of date features as a tapering off of your interest in her. Each one of the withdrawals might not be that bad by itself, but together, they form a classic case of death by pinprick. Death by pinprick refers to a person being pricked multiple times, and while the impact of each prick is insignificant, the cumulative impact can be lethal. She might notice the change immediately but wait a few weeks before accepting that things have changed. Once she realizes that some of the attention she was getting earlier is gone, how do you think she will feel? My guess is that she will not be excited.

Do You Not Love Me Anymore?

Recently, when I was flying on my regular airline and got a complimentary upgrade to first class, I was kind of elated. I sat down and nearly got lost in the 75 percent larger seats, and I stretched my legs to enjoy the amazing amount of legroom. After the flight took off, I got out my laptop and started working. Soon the flight attendant came over to ask me what I wanted to drink. Before bringing the beverage, the attendant brought a tiny yet cute cup of mixed nuts. I always look forward to warm mixed nuts and savor them one piece at a time. As I was typing, my left hand left the keyboard and went to the nuts; I took the first nut and put it in my mouth. As I tried the second one, I realized that something was different. The nuts were cold. They were not my regular warm, toasted nuts, and that bummed me out. I felt that switching the nuts was not fair, as I liked those mixed nuts served warm.

As I was reflecting on the changed condition of my mixed nuts, my coffee arrived. This was a surprise too. It was not in the regular porcelain cup that I hold with both hands and feel the warmth before I drink. Instead, it was a foam cup. Now I was seriously worried. First, the toasted nuts were no longer warm, and now the coffee cup was different. What else had my airline done behind my back? I started looking at everything with a tinge of suspicion. Soon the seat started to feel less comfortable, the restroom seemed tinier, and the salad they served was no longer fulfilling. Then, when the entertainment started on the television and an advertisement for the airline came on, I shook my head in denial and said, "Nope, not true. You have changed behind my back." All these doubts crept in because they had not warmed the mixed nuts and had used a foam cup instead of a porcelain cup.

I guess shortcuts define the brand in the mind of the customers. When customers catch a brand taking some shortcuts, they then view all elements of the brand with suspicion. The reverse of this also holds true. If a brand surprises customers with something nice and then follows it with something else that is a pleasant surprise, soon the customers will start to wonder if everything the brand is offering is new and improved.

The airline industry has been going through immense cost-cutting measures in the last few years. In the background of cost cutting, it is easy to infer that the airlines are going through a transition from a hospitality industry to a retail transportation industry. Earlier, it was all about hospitality, which included greeting passengers at the door, assisting the elderly to their seats, getting the customers pillows and blankets, and offering refreshments that included meals, snacks, and beverages.

Somehow, in the process of cost cutting, first, the free food disappeared. Then some financial genius measured the aggregate payload carried by airplanes as a result of all the magazine weight, resulting in the higher fuel cost, and hence, the complimentary magazines vanished. Then the peanuts and pretzels went away, and the airlines started using captive hungry customers as a revenue-generating opportunity by selling food. If that is not the first step to retail, I do not know what retail is.

As airlines continue in this format, the big question is the evolving role of flight attendants. Why do I still need them to say good-bye as I exit the airplane? Why do they continue the farcical service of walking down the aisle with water once in a three-hour flight? Why not be consistent and completely be a retail service? In that case, the role of the flight attendant becomes more of an enforcer, similar to the ticket collector on a train. We do not expect the ticket collector to get us pillows, do we?

To be consistent, maybe the airlines should put vending machines on the plane, change the flight attendant uniforms from hospitality aprons to service jumpsuits, and offer great retail service but not try to be in the hospitality industry. Customers might appreciate the honesty. Then, if some airlines want to stand out and offer hospitality the old-fashioned way, that would be a true brand differentiator. Be true to what you stand for, whether in dates or customer acquisition.

I believe that even under these difficult changing conditions, a team member can touch the heart of a customer and make a huge impact. Here is an example, again from the airline industry. Although the team member was in a no-win situation, she saved the day for the airline.

Creating Magic out of Nothing

As I mentioned earlier, lately, there has been hardly any food on flights, even in first class. On this particular trip, even though I was upgraded to first class, to avoid the frustration of being hungry during the flight, I stopped at a Mexican fast-food restaurant and got a taco salad before boarding my flight. After I boarded the flight and sat down in my seat, the flight attendant saw me with my fast-food bag and teased, "Can I have it?"

My immediate reaction with a smile was "Nope! It is mine!"

She smiled and said that since I was in the first row, I could not have a food bag on my lap or in front of me during takeoff. She then took my salad and carefully placed it in one of the stainless steel bins for takeoff. I watched her closely and was not sure if I should approve of her actions.

As the flight reached cruising altitude and the seat belt lights turned off, she came over, opened my table for me, and put a linen tablecloth on it. Then she carefully brought my salad to me with another glass of water. The white linen, the silverware, and the fact that I was the only person enjoying this salad made this a special dinner. It was no longer a taco salad from a Mexican fast-food place; instead, it was a gourmet meal. I thanked the flight attendant, as her level of service and desire to make my flight a wow-inducing experience was no less than that of a renowned Nordstrom team member or a waiter in a high-end restaurant.

I kept thinking about the limited resources she had with her on the plane. Instead of complaining about the airline not giving her the opportunity to provide wow-inducing guest service, she took it upon herself to make the best out of the situation and put customers first. Inside her was a strong desire to go above and beyond for the customer. Wow.

In this case, the team member single-handedly created a brand experience that built on the brand's image. Hence, the actions of team members have the potential to define a brand. The halos created by individual acts can define a brand perception. When I realized that the mixed nuts were no longer warm and the coffee was being served in a foam cup, I immediately started suspecting the airlines of taking other shortcuts, but when the flight attendant transformed my airport fast food into a special meal, that one act made me fall in love with the airline. It is amazing to see how the customer mind gets influenced.

This shows that customers are human beings with emotions. Anytime a brand gives something to the customer on an ongoing basis to appreciate the customer, the customer looks at that as an entitlement instead of an appreciation for the brand. Hence, it is important to do the following:

1. Set clear expectations right from the beginning. Define clearly the experience elements that the customer can continue to expect every time and the special add-on gestures from the brand.
2. When an experience element changes or a service element is withdrawn, a brand must proactively communicate with the customers and inform them of the change. That information, with some explanation, might prevent customers from getting irate.
3. Anything that is extra should be positioned as a gift of appreciation to the customer. The brand must take credit for it and make the customer realize that not everyone gets this. That will make the customer appreciate the gift and feel special.

Texting "XOXO" in the Middle of the Night

When I was growing up, my grandma taught me that appropriateness is defined by doing the right thing at the right time. Does that mean that in the case of showing affection to a customer, there can be a wrong time? I believe so. Let me review this airline example.

Midnight Text to Show Appreciation

The airline I fly most on has started treating me nicely. I have flown more than one hundred thousand miles in each of the last five calendar years. The airline has given me a special phone number, and when I call and punch in my ten-digit frequent-flier number, I get access to an operator without a long wait. I get to board the plane first, and often, I get upgraded to first class free of charge. As I mentioned earlier, the free upgrade is something that I look forward to. I am not sure if this is because of the service in first class or the lack of service in coach. Today there is no food served in coach, and those who get a full can of Diet Coke instead of a glass should feel lucky. The seating comfort, service level, and shorter line for the restroom all make me look forward to a first-class upgrade.

Over time, the airline started informing me two to three days before my flight about the upgrade. However, one thing bothered me: the timing of the message. Every time, without fail, they sent me text messages in the middle of the night. Do you think a free upgrade, however much I look forward to it, is worth waking me up and telling me, "You got upgraded. Happy? Now go back to sleep, knowing that your favorite airline loves you and is thinking of you"? Not really!

Let me tell you what goes through my mind. First of all, I do not turn my phone off at night, as my mom lives in India, and I want her to be able to access me anytime she wants to. When I abruptly wake up at the sound of the airline's text and try to find my phone, I worry if my mom is okay in India. When I finally find my phone and check the message, I am relieved that it is my airline and not any bad news from India. I read the message, get up, go to the restroom, and come back to bed. My girlfriend, who has also been woken up, will ask me, "Is everything all right?" and I will tell her, "It is my airline telling me that I have been upgraded." As I say that, even to me, it is difficult to believe. She is kind, but I worry that in her mind, she is saying, *Hmm, sure. Of course it was the airline!* In today's dating world, one's cell phone is usually out of reach of one's partner. But there are times when I am tempted to show her the screen of my phone and say, "Look. It is the airline who sent me the text. It is not some strange woman texting me in the middle of the night."

I am not calling my airline insensitive. I think they find it efficient to run the upgrades when the system is at its lowest use, which is clearly in the middle of the night. From an operator's point of view, it is an efficient use of resources. But shouldn't they think for a second that I and other frequent fliers are humans, and most of us usually sleep at that time? I love the gift of love from my airline, but to me, the timing of the gift is inappropriate.

They should put themselves in my shoes and incorporate a no-texting policy between ten o'clock at night and six o'clock in the morning unless there is a flight delay; in that case, I do not mind them waking me up to tell me that my 6:00 a.m. flight is not taking off until 10:00 a.m. But please don't text me in the middle of the night to tell me that I am upgraded. Trust me—I will appreciate this news more when I am awake.

This is true in every industry outside the airline industry and in your personal life. Visualize that you and your spouse are in the middle of a deep conversation as you are out for dinner. The manager comes in; stands in front of you, in a place where he can clearly hear both of you speak; and says, "I am the manager of the restaurant and wanted to thank you in person for coming in today. I see you ordered the chicken marsala and chopped chicken salad. How was it? Is everything okay? Is there anything I can do for you?" Of course, you say, "No, thank you," but what you meant to say was "Bad timing, dude! You just interrupted our date."

The wrong timing makes customers think that the brand is insensitive to their needs. You don't even call your best friend in the middle of the night unless it is an emergency. Hence, proper timing for customer appreciation is necessary to build a stronger relationship with the customer. The solution to finding the right timing is an extension of a previous chapter in which I talked about giving the gift of love and not what you can afford to give. The answer is again the same: empower the team members to figure out when to wow the customer, one customer at a time. Even the best gifts given at the wrong time can be bad karma. Marketing should educate operations team members about the lives of customers so that they can intervene at the right time.

My Pleasure? Really?

When a customer thanks you, how you respond can influence your connection with the brand. I feel it is essential that one is always authentic and true to him- or herself during any communication. That is true for any gesture in a relationship. You might be dating someone who plays it perfectly by the book. He brings flowers to you on every date, and after a date, he sends you a nice card, but you keep feeling that something is missing. You think for days and finally realize that all these gestures are happening mechanically, as if the person is following a playbook of dating. He is not putting his heart into it and not personalizing things. You feel he is putting a lot of effort into checking the right boxes, and when you look at things rationally, you appreciate his efforts, but the emotional connection is lacking. In any relationship, rational and emotional connections are needed.

In the business world, doing what seems to be required without true feeling for the recipient is common. You have experienced employees greeting you mechanically within minutes of your entering a store, without pausing for eye contact. You have experienced a manager in a fancy restaurant coming to the table, asking if everything is all right, and not even waiting for you to complete your answer. Maybe you have left an auto repair place and had the manager give you a survey to fill out and mail back, insisting that you put 10s on every question, as his team's bonus depends on this. Now, is that the real reason the feedback system was put in place? The reason a business started the welcome greeting or the manager stop-by, for example, was to make the customer feel welcome and to fix any customer problems during the dinner itself.

Learning How to Say "My Pleasure"

The reason employees greet you mechanically became clear to me when I was working on a project to enhance a brand's customer experience. As

I was trying to identify who did the best job at the end of the experience, the name that came up consistently was Chick-fil-A. Team members at Chick-fil-A were perceived to be the best available in the trade area and were defined by their signature response to a customer saying, "Thank you." They always said, "My pleasure." As I'm an eternal disbeliever, I had to go to a Chick-fil-A immediately. Every time I said thank you, I received the "My pleasure" response. I went to different Chick-fil-A restaurants, and there was consistency in the expression of "My pleasure." Finally, I was convinced that this was the definition of Chick-fil-A-ness and was not a random occurrence at Chick-fil-A. They had created a culture of customer-centric team members who truly meant that it was their pleasure to serve the customer.

Next, I wanted to compare how other brands in different industries responded to a thank-you. I started with a high-end retail store, and the response to my thank-you was again "My pleasure," but something did not sound right. I again said, "Thank you," and I got an automated repeat response of "My pleasure." I realized that this team member had been conditioned to say "My pleasure" like a robot when he heard "Thank you," similar to when a person says, "Bless you," when someone sneezes. To the best of my knowledge, that kind of automatic "Bless you" does not usually mean a sincere religious blessing. This automatic response is also similar to the dating example in which the man always brought flowers to a date but never connected emotionally with his date.

I embarked on a personal journey to return to the "My pleasure" university, Chick-fil-A. After countless "My pleasures," I learned that Chick-fil-A's "My pleasure" had the following associated with it.

- The team member smiled as he or she said, "My pleasure."
- There was a pause after I said, "Thank you." To me, it felt as if the team member heard the words, the words went to his or her heart, and then a "My pleasure" emerged from there.

Then I went back to the retail store and watched the employees closely. I witnessed that even though I was standing in front of the team member, there was no eye contact, smile, or pause, and there was an automatic utterance of "My pleasure." Next, I performed this test during every retail, service, hospitality, and restaurant experience and wrote down the responses I got. The top two responses to "Thank you" as I performed my little research project were "No problem" and "Uh-huh." Here were my personal feelings and reactions when I heard each of the responses.

- "No problem": I know there is not a problem. I paid in full for this and even added a tip. Were you expecting a problem? Like what?
- "Uh-huh": Can you not speak coherently in a language that I understand? Was that an acknowledgment of receipt of my thank-you?
- "My pleasure": I was expecting a Chick-fil-A-level "My pleasure," and in most cases, the responses fell short. I felt that one should not say, "My pleasure," unless he or she meant it. The lack of insincerity was too transparent.
- "Sure": This was similar to "No problem" but a tad softer.
- "Anytime": This response had a positive side. Delivered properly, it created a halo of a problem solver ready to help. I liked it.
- "You're welcome": This was nice too, but somehow, my bias was toward "My pleasure."
- A smile with no verbal response: This was similar to "Uh-huh" but was without the attitude. When delivered with eye contact, a smile felt truly reassuring.
- "You should take a survey and tell my supervisor": This came across as calculating and self-centered. But as I thought more, I realized that it was not the fault of the team member; it was the system of incentives set up around him or her.
- "Mention it not": This was a British response and again implied that I deserved and was entitled to the service and that a thank-you was not necessary. The response came across as abrupt, but when I rationalized it, it made sense to me.
- "Fine": This made me feel that the team member approved my saying, "Thank you." It was baffling.

- "Absolutely" and "Of course": Again, I did not know how "Absolutely" or "Of course" could be a response to "Thank you," but when I heard it, based on the confidence with which it was delivered, something in it felt right. Hence, even though I cannot rationally explain the reason, emotionally, it got me engaged.
- "Anything else I can do?": This was my favorite response. I was at an Asian grocery store, where I was trying to find some things, and an elderly team member walked with me and helped me find what I was looking for. Finally, when I was ready to leave the store, I walked over to her and said, "Thank you." She took my hands, smiled, and said softly, "Anything else I can do? If not, the next time you are back in the store, come find me. I would like to help you anytime." This time, I paused. I had no response; I just smiled back. Of course, what went through my mind was *You had me at your smile and handshake.*

When I started reflecting back on all the responses, I felt that in most cases, the team members seemed to be in a rush—to go back to work, attend to the next customer, or do something else that was more important than listening to me say, "Thank you." The rush made me feel that I was an interruption rather than a valued guest. This rush is universal, be it with a retail outlet, restaurant, or service provider. What is the cause of this universal rush?

As I mentioned earlier, this is an interesting area that a lot of brands miss. When a customer is really touched by a brand and initiates a contact, a sincere, authentic response from the brand moves the relationship forward. On the other hand, if there is an abrupt, impersonal response, it freezes the customer and dampens his or her enthusiasm. All brands have to do is take a few extra seconds to connect with the customer and finish the experience strong, and in the process, they will build the relationship.

Start with Authenticity

When a brand tries to trick a customer, it is relying on its chances of not getting caught. The consequence of getting caught is the loss of a lifetime of a relationship. But more importantly, when a brand tries to trick a customer, it disrespects the intelligence of the customer, thinking the customer is not smart enough to figure it out. That is never going to make the customer feel good. Relationships are natural and spontaneous when both partners have nothing to hide and are just their normal selves. In that mind-set, when one does good karma that touches the other person, he or she is likely to be rewarded with good karma in return. Without authenticity, a customer will not build a long-term relationship with a company.

Authenticity is a must in any relationship and comes from two main areas.

1. **Being True to Yourself:** This means being who you are and not trying to be someone else.

2. **Following the Golden Rule:** The golden rule states that you should treat others the way you want others to treat you. This rule is comprehensive, as following this alone consistently makes a brand authentic in its interactions.

No Room for Trick Play

Let me start with an everyday example and see if it is good karma or not. In our daily lives, we often get caught in the traps and tricks of different businesses around us.

Mazes in Home Improvement Stores

Think of the last time you visited a home improvement store. These are usually big units with thousands of square feet. As you entered the parking lot and started looking for a parking spot, you faced a dilemma. The question that popped up in your mind was "Where should I park?" You could see two signs, Enter and Exit, clearly marked on the storefront. But they were on two corners of the parking lot. Let's say you were feeling a bit lazy and chose to park near the Enter sign. You walked in, took your time shopping, and then, finally, half an hour later, came out of the store, pushing a cartload of stuff you had purchased.

When you left the store, you realized you were not at the same door you entered. All of a sudden, you panicked. You decided to retrace your steps to your original entry point, hoping to identify the exact spot where you parked. You pushed the cartload of purchases through the parking lot for a few minutes. Eventually, you resorted to the final approach that you badly wanted to avoid: you took out your car keys and started clicking on the lock and unlock buttons to try to hear your car calling out to you. Finally, you found the car, walked over, and loaded your purchases. As you got into the driver's seat, you shook your head in disbelief. You kept thinking how silly it was that you were unable to locate your car in a parking lot. At that moment, you heard another car beeping in the parking lot. You were slightly relieved that you were not the only one to get lost. You were happy that you did not press the panic button. As I reflect on how your seemingly simple visit to a home improvement store turned out to be a not-so-simple event, I have to admit that the experience was not one to make a person say, "Wow."

Those operating the store might have their reasons for the layout. Having the same entrance and exit could cause accidental bumps, because the store sells large items, such as big wooden planks. Eliminating this risk is ideal, and the risk is almost entirely gone when the store removes the two-way traffic. From a security point of view, if all customers must exit from another area, the store can easily keep an eye on them. Having a different entrance and exit creates a circular flow of people throughout the store. Circular flow is a concept that operations textbooks preach, because it creates a natural in-store customer flow and maximum efficiency.

Alone in the Movie Theater Parking Lot

In the case of movie theaters, you often enter through the main entrance and then leave through a back door at the end of the movie. This flow pattern makes it simple to check customers' tickets as they enter. If crowds of customers coming out of the theater and entering the theater converge at the same time at the same entrance, checking tickets could be a nightmare. This is another example of a brand achieving a higher level of efficiency by planning the customer flow.

Let me take a step back to assess the cost of all these efficiencies in customer flow. They all came at the expense of making customers feel stupid when some of them were unable to find their cars in the parking lot. At the movie theater, viewers were forced to exit from the back of the building and found themselves in a dimly lit parking lot in the middle of the night, somewhat unsure of their safety as they cautiously navigated back to their cars. Let's compare this to the dating example. You start the date with a bang; you have roses and a big smile. At the end of the date, you see it is raining, and your date tells you that she is parked three blocks away. You give her a half hug and wish her good night.

It would have been nice if you had gotten an umbrella and walked her to the car. That, to me, was the right thing to do and was the right karma.

In the example using the home improvement store, customers were also forced to wander around the store while pushing carts filled with heavy items. In the process, customers might have picked up some extra batteries, hand sanitizers, candy bars, or a few other items they had no intention of buying. Those purchases were the result of the store successfully tricking them, at least on this visit.

Finally, when customers got back to their cars and looked at the well-lit signage of the store, what did they feel? Did they completely forget about the parking lot disorientation they just experienced? Did they feel good or slightly worn out after being unnecessarily forced to walk around? Did they feel somewhat tricked as they glanced at the extra items they bought in the store? With all these negative feelings, as customers looked at the store's signage one last time before leaving the parking lot, did they think, *I cannot wait to come back*? Or did they roll their eyes, shake their heads, and think, *I cannot believe what you did to me*? Whatever customers' feelings were, they survived on their terms and headed out into the world to live their lives.

Inside the store, the store team had a lot of control over the customers' actions, but after leaving the store, the customers had total control regarding what to tell their friends about their experience. Customers also had full control over whether or not they wanted to return to the same store the next time. The store should have remembered that during the customers' visits to the store. As each customer chose the store to find the solutions he or she sought, it was important for the store to be appreciative of the trust it received and act accordingly. The store should have focused on being authentic and finding the best way to offer the customer a solution, not on trying to make a few extra dollars from the customer during his or her visit to the store. To me, the latter is not good customer karma at all. The power completely transitions to the customers the moment they leave the store, and the customer always uses the power based on the experience in the store.

Winning Strategy

Here's what the store could have done differently if all team members were aligned and they put their customers' needs first.

1. If the store had to have a different entry and exit, they should have marked the parking lot clearly and communicated to the customer that he or she was parked in row C, spot 34. They could have put scanning signs on each parking space for the customers to quickly record their parking locations. They also could have taken extra care to make the customers aware as they entered the store that the exit was in a different place.
2. The store could have placed a kiosk at the entry to aid the customer in finding the one exact item that he or she was looking for. That way, the customer could have gone directly to that item and then made a straight dash for the exit. The store could have taken this strategy even further by providing smartphone apps that allowed the customers to shop while sitting in their cars and then navigated them through the store to pick the items. This process also would have informed a customer if the items he or she was looking for were in stock or out of stock.

There are numerous other things the store could have done, and any one of them would have resulted in good karma if they'd put the customer first. Automatically putting the customer first would have guided all the decisions in the right spirit of serving the customer and offered the customer the solution he or she was seeking when coming to the store. The customers too would have responded, as they would have clearly gotten that the store was trying its best to respect their time and make their shopping easy.

Here is a simple way to test if an idea is or is not customer-centric. The store team should think of the customer as a good friend of theirs. Maybe even give the friend a name (e.g., Jane Doe). Next, they should imagine that Jane had come to them, the store team, with a particular problem or need. At that point, the store team could focus all their attention on solving their friend Jane's problem. This attention would make Jane an even closer friend and maybe a lifetime friend. Or the store team could seize the opportunity to have Jane as a captive audience with no escape and try to sell her insurance and other items before offering a solution to her problem. Of course, if the store team did this, Jane would feel that the members of the store team were not good friends, and that friendship would be bound to get weaker. Only bad karma would result.

In simple terms, a store should be grateful that in today's world, with millions of choices, a customer came to them seeking a solution. The store team opens the store every day in anticipation of this opportunity, and once the opportunity arrives, offering a customer-centric solution should be their priority.

This total, undivided attention seems to be a simple concept in relationships, so why are most businesses not doing this? As the economy gets tougher, more and more companies are moving their focus to short-term gains. This short-term-gain focus makes the companies try to get more and more time and money out of customers when they get them into the store. Most of these short-term-focused companies believe in the business theory "If there is no short term, there is no long term." But is this a sustainable business model? Do they have a long-term business model based on tricking the customer? They might think that customers are all right as long as they are not terribly inconvenienced, but that is wrong. Customers have felt compromised for too long and have tolerated these actions by businesses rather than considering them to be acceptable. It is just a matter of time until some smart brand figures all this out and offers the customer a better solution; then the customer will sit back and ask, "What was I thinking?" This risk, or opportunity, is precisely the reason I put this line on the cover of the book: "Why stop at a one-night stand, when you can have a lifetime relationship with your customers?"

All businesses must realize that an average customer spends much more time between visits to their business than in the store. A restaurant visit might take one hour, but the customer takes a few weeks before returning.

A grocery store visit might take twenty minutes, but a customer takes two to three days before the next visit. During the time away, customers have lives. In their personal lives, customers have control of their actions and decisions. Therefore, if you put the customer first when he or she is visiting your business, then when the customer is away, that good karma will create a positive perception in the customer's mind. That positive perception will strengthen the customer's relationship with the brand and bring him or her back more often.

Can't Believe You Made Me Feel Stupid

This personal favorite topic of mine is based on the following concept: "The customer is smart and deserves respect for that."

If you look at any industry, you will find examples of a customer being made to feel somewhat stupid. It might not be intentional, but a brand must identify these moments on its own and solve them, as it is tough to build a long-term, loyal relationship with a customer if the relationship starts with the brand making him or her feel stupid.

Here are a few examples.

- After a long day of travel, you get to your hotel, and once you enter the dark room, dragging all your luggage with you, you cannot find the light switch.
- You come to a new restaurant and keep trying to figure out where to go to place an order.
- You get to a doctor's office, and they ask you for all your old records.
- You are on a retail brand's website, trying in vain to find out the location nearest to you.
- You call a business and have to listen to the full set of voice instructions to figure out all the options they provide. Finally, when you get a chance to press the button to make your choice, you are not sure and have to listen to the full recording again.
- This example might not sound difficult when you are reading it, but when you are in the actual situation, you might feel unsure and uncomfortable. When you are at a sit-down restaurant, you order your entrée. Next, the server asks you what three sides you want.

Is the restaurant telling you that they take pride in preparing for you any side you are in the mood to eat? Or are they testing you to see if you read the list of side items that are usually hidden in some corner of the menu?

- Finally, consider a car rental example. You fly in late and get to the rental car counter. The agent is friendly and processes your reservation efficiently. He then hands you the car rental contract in a paper jacket, with the car's location written on the jacket. As you walk out to the car rental parking lot to locate your car, you look at the jacket. Is it 701 or 101? Or is it 262 or 202? Or is it 445, 495, or 995? Today, as we mostly type rather than write, the emphasis on good handwriting is vanishing. Hence, it is common to get confused between a 7 and a 1, a 6 and a 0, or a 4 and a 9. In fact, if your car is in space 796, eight different options could be the right spot, and at eleven o'clock at night, most business travelers don't want to use the clues from the unclear handwriting to play the game of figuring out where the car is.

The emotion felt by the guest in each of these examples lasts for only a short period, but the intensity of the negative emotion is strong; that intensity is bound to make a negative impact on the emotional connection of customer with the brand. Brands must realize that customers are human beings and come to the brand for total solutions. Here are a few examples of times when the person you are dating can feel awkward on a date.

- You have invited your date to come with you to a family gathering. This visit is the first time she is going to meet a lot of friends and family. Once both of you get to the gathering, if you leave her alone to find your high school buddies, she might be standing in one place, feeling uncomfortable.
- You choose a restaurant for the second date. Your date is a vegan, and you knew it on the first date. As both of you sit down and get ready to order, you realize that the only things she can order are different side items or a chicken salad without the chicken.

- After a date, you give her a hug and walk to your car. You do not realize that she parked two blocks away, and when she gets there, she realizes that she has a flat tire. She calls for help, and as she waits for help to arrive, she feels disappointed that the date ended this way.
- You are an avid golfer, and she has never golfed before. You invite her to your golf club so both of you can hit balls on the range. Once she shows up, she realizes that she is not wearing the appropriate clothes for golf.

Similar to the guest, your date feels strong negative, uncomfortable emotions for a short period, as you jump in and fix the situation quickly. But because the intensity of the negative emotions is high, they do not just go away. The aftertaste of the awkwardness lingers and might impact how your date emotionally connects to you. Rationally, she appreciates that you jumped in and solved the problem, but the emotional awkwardness does not simply go away.

This is a clear extension of the golden rule, as both the customer and the date should be treated in a way the other party expects to be treated. Awareness of the situation the customer is in, including what he or she needs and how he or she wants to be treated, is essential in order to make the customer not feel stupid or ignored.

Surprises from Friends and Family

Brands spend millions of dollars trying to influence customers' perceptions. It is the perception that is a reality. However, customers often take what brands say with a grain of salt. This distrust is magnified in the United States, as in this country, it is legal to use puffery in advertising. Therefore, if a brand makes a claim that is outrageous, then the onus is on the customer to decipher and figure out that the claim is not true. For example, if I made the claim in my advertising that I am the world's best basketball player, then it is for you to figure out that I am stretching the truth. But if I say that I am better than Michael Jordan or LeBron James, then I have to furnish proof. Either way, many times, the puffery sets an expectation in the mind of the customer that brands stretch the truth, so customers do not fully believe what a brand says.

On the other hand, things a brand does that the customer notices create a halo effect. Recently, I was passing a new fast-food restaurant in an airport and saw the following message posted: "Today's potatoes are from the Roberts' farm in Idaho." That message gives the brand a halo of credibility and freshness that permeates all aspects of the brand experience. All this is good until the customer gets excited and walks up to the cash register. He tells the team member, "It is so cool that you guys get the potatoes from the Roberts' farm in Idaho. I grew up a few miles from them." At that point, the team member can do one of the following.

1. He or she can share with excitement the details of the potatoes and how they are used to make the best fries. This happens only if marketing has already shared details about the potatoes and additional information with every team member. The operations team member enjoys telling a more detailed story of the potatoes.

2. If he or she has no clue about where the potatoes come from or why they are different, he or she can look at the poster and try to wing an answer.
3. He or she can choose to not answer the question and simply move on to what the customer owes.
4. He or she can smile and murmur, "That is marketing propaganda. You and I both know that all potatoes are the same."

The first response would build on the marketing story and become a big wow factor for the customer; the last answer would discredit the marketing story and become a big whoa. So the simple difference between a wow and a whoa is whether or not marketing takes the time to educate operations about the marketing message in advance and whether or not employees take the time to understand the details of the marketing promotion. Together, marketing and operations can either make or break any promotion.

Just as brands like to build their perceptions, humans, during a dating phase, try to build our perceptions. What one says on the online dating site and on the date creates a perception in the other person's mind. Think of a situation in which you and your date are hanging out with your buddies, watching a football game. You and your date have learned a lot about each other, and she is impressed with you and your past accomplishments. As all of you are hanging out, your date casually mentions to one of your buddies how impressed she is that you were a star football player in high school. At that point, your buddy can do one of the following.

1. He starts talking about your high school football days. In this case, her perception gets reinforced, and she starts admiring you even more.
2. He stumbles and tries to be a good friend by winging an answer. She smiles and realizes that you exaggerated but is happy that you have good friends who will stand by you.
3. He looks at her, surprised, and says, "Hmm, really?" This answer breaks your credibility. Your date immediately starts wondering what else you have shared with her that is not credible.

In the same way, how many times have you seen something advertised, gone to the store, and asked for the special, only to have a store team member look at you as if you were from a different planet? How many times have you seen an advertisement in which the brand brags about how its processes and ingredients are different, gone to the store, and asked a team member, only to get the same "Really? Get outta here" look?

Please Help Me Buy the Gadget I Need

Here is a personal story that happened when I was at an electronics retailer and saw four different GPS products advertised, each with a detailed description. I loved all four and went to the store to buy one for my daughter, who had just started to drive. When I went to the store, I realized that the four-by-six-inch card of information in front of each GPS said less than what I knew, so I called for help. The specialist who came to help me was a confident young man with a great smile, and he was full of energy. But his first question worried me. He said, "Hmm, they've advertised these products in the weekly flyer?" I had no idea what that question meant and wondered if I'd made a mistake in coming to this retailer for this product. However, then he got into the details of the information to help me choose. He started reading each card, and then he would get excited about a feature in a particular GPS. He paraphrased the importance of that feature and then read the other GPS information to me, only to be disheartened to find that the other ones had the same feature. This went on for nearly five minutes. Finally, he admitted that they all were nearly the same and said I should buy the one that was the cheapest. Of course, I left the store without buying anything and felt I'd wasted my time.

Another time, when a favorite restaurant of mine started advertising about its vegetables being all organic, in my excitement, I asked the restaurant staff member what was natural about the restaurant's ingredients. She was clueless. Her response was "I did not know our ingredients are natural. They come in a truck just like any other ingredients, and we do not get them from Whole Foods."

Hmm, I said to myself, *that was not what I was expecting.* I was waiting for the team member to jump up and down with pride and describe to me why she was proud to work with a restaurant that went to that level to serve what was the best. In this case, I do not doubt the truth in the advertising, but if team members do not support and reinforce the claim made in the advertisement, it casts a shadow of doubt in the customer's mind about the claim's credibility, especially when a team member shows ignorance about the advertising.

One Special Potato from Idaho

All advertising statements start as self-bragging. To me, they only set expectations or tickle curiosity. In the end, a brand's promise is realized when a customer interacts with the team members and the products. If team members are not educated and informed, customers will wonder if they are making the right decision. On the other hand, a team member who is a die-hard customer of the brand and is excited about the differences mentioned in the advertising is a great brand messenger. Hence, when you roll out a new idea, please make sure that you educate first your internal team and then the rest of the world. That will make it easy for you when customers start coming in. The enthusiasm of the team members will augment the message in the advertising, and that combination will make the customer feel good about visiting your brand. Here is a simple yet fun way a fast-food restaurant can get team members excited about the potatoes from the Roberts' farm in Idaho. They could announce that the employee of the month in each market gets a three-day trip to Boise, Idaho. Two of the days could be sightseeing and spa visits in Boise, and the third day would be a visit to the Roberts' farm in Idaho to experience the family potato farm. When the employees returned, their experience with the potatoes from the Roberts' farm in Idaho would go further than just the potato poster in the restaurant in generating excitement among employees.

Brands need to be aware of the reality and educate employees on the brand's promise before talking to the customer. In the case of dating, it is slightly different; it would be smart for a person to stay with the facts and limit the glorification of the facts.

Strategizing Not to Get Caught

Nearly everyone faces shortcuts in life that can make things more efficient. Sometimes brands find clever shortcuts that the customer does not care about but that are big wins for the brands. In such cases, a brand must take time to understand how the short-term gains will impact the brand in the long term. Sometimes the long-term wins can be significant, but does it matter what the value of the win is before one chooses a take a shortcut?

Pepperoni Vanishing from a Pizza

Let me create a situation for you, and you decide how you would act in this case.

- You are the CEO of a national pizza brand with nearly $1 billion in annual sales.
- You are looking for ways to increase sales and increase profitability every day.
- An external vendor has come up with the promise of $21-million-a-year cost savings. Here is their three-step plan.
    - Pizza A: They have tested a new, thinner pepperoni, and based on sensory tests, current customers could not find any difference between pizza A and the current product.
    - Pizza B: They recommend that in one year, you switch to pizza B, which features a new way of arranging the pepperoni whereby fifty-seven pepperoni instead of sixty give the same coverage. "The same coverage" is defined by the fact that customers found no difference between the pizza A with sixty thinner pepperoni and the pizza B with fifty-seven thinner pepperoni.

- Pizza C: They recommend that in another year, you go to pizza C, which will feature slightly smaller pepperoni. Again, based on sensory tests, customers could not find any difference between pizza C's fifty-seven smaller, thinner pepperoni and the other pizza toppings.

What would you do? Shouldn't you go for the win-win solution, as it is a cost-saving option that has no downside for customers?

Brands go through situations like this often. As I look at this money-saving opportunity, I have some questions.

1. If you have to get to pizza C eventually, why not go to it directly? Does that mean that customers in a sensory test see that both pizza B and pizza C are different from the current pizza recipe? Hence, the step-by-step approach is a way to make sure that the customer does not see the change?
2. Even if the sensory test shows customers did not find any changes in the pizzas, an individual customer might feel that the pepperoni on the pizza is different and ask a store what changed in the pepperoni pizza. Would the brand share with the customer that they have found a way to make same pizza using less pepperoni?

This example is a classic example of death by pinprick, where one makes small, undiscovered changes from year to year, and then, all of a sudden, the product is significantly different from the original.

I computed that pizza C will have approximately 11 percent fewer pepperoni on every pizza. Even though I had only three data points over a two-and-half-year period, if the same trend continued, then here is what the weight of the pepperoni on the pizza would look like over the years:

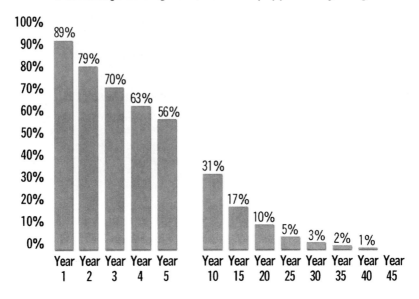

Based on the projection, in five years, a pepperoni pizza would only have 56 percent of today's amount of pepperoni; in ten years, it would have 31 percent; in twenty years, it would have 10 percent; and after thirty years, there would be hardly any pepperoni left on the pizza. This type of iterative cost saving can directly destroy a brand. Hence, without a comparison to a gold standard, how can a company make sure it doesn't fall into this trap?

The brand's decision to move forward with this strategy will depend upon the fact that customers cannot see any difference in the pizza. This concept of successfully getting away with something behind customers' backs cannot result in a big customer win. Please note that the changes are not illegal.

When a brand goes for this kind of short-term-profit win, the brand does not have any customer win; in fact, there is a high probability of serious customer loss in the long term. Therefore, there is no good customer karma at any point, and there is hardly any potential for a long-term win with the customer. If there is no good customer karma, why do brands pursue this path? The answer is often in an understanding of management compensation. If the management team's bonus is based on short-term profitability and not long-term success, it is plausible that the management team will choose the short-term win. However, we should not blame management teams alone. I feel that if a brand's bonus is connected to short-term wins, then it is tough for management team members to look beyond the short term. There needs to be an alignment of brand vision, compensation, and evaluation all through an organization to maintain the long-term health of the brand and the brand experience.

In the dating world, this is equivalent to a person who intentionally partially discloses an event to mislead his or her partner. For example, a man realizes that if his partner gets to know everything that happened last weekend, it could mean the end of the relationship. Hence, he chooses to share a little bit at a time over time to minimize the shock. In this case, the picture gets clearer than the pizza example. The person apparently knows the consequence of disclosing all the facts at once, and he has consciously planned the partial disclosure to get away with something. I feel that any time there is an action with the intent to hide, it breaks trust and relationships.

In the case of both the business relationship and the romantic relationship, what the brand or the individual is doing is not illegal. However, each clearly comes across as someone who cannot be trusted, and in the journey for a lifetime relationship, lack of trust does not help the brand. The customer might still use the brand, but once he or she finds out that the brand cannot be trusted, that discovery can be a relationship killer.

A Warm Heart Always Gets Noticed

I just talked about brands that come across as entities that cannot be trusted. Now let us talk about brands that are good at heart.

Being a good citizen should come from a brand's heart and be spontaneous. This cannot be a program and should be in a brand's DNA. A brand needs to go beyond treating customers the right way. The brand needs to be a good citizen, be caring and considerate, and do its fair share of investing in the brand. To start, let me ask you how you feel in each of the following examples.

Eighteen-Wheeler Delivery Truck in the Neighborhood

In the morning, as you walk your twin daughters to the bus stop, an eighteen-wheeler, a delivery truck for a supermarket, drives through the neighborhood. This does not give you a good feeling, I bet. You must be wondering, *Shouldn't they know that young children go to school at this time? Why can't they plan deliveries in the middle of the night, when the kids are not out on the streets?*

Distributing Coupons at a High School Track Meet

In this example, a local restaurant chain representative is giving out coupons at a high school track meet. Again, this will not give you a positive feeling. You might think, *How did you know that we would be gathering here this evening? What else do you know about me? Shouldn't the school track be a commercial-free zone?* Even if I finally came to terms with the fact that there are no sacred, commercial-free zones left on the planet, I would still ask the restaurant chain, "What is in it for the high school?" It is clear that the restaurant is gaining by using the event as a local marketing opportunity. Shouldn't the restaurant reciprocate by feeding the athletes after the meet?

Carnations at a Funeral

The next example is a tough one that is close to me. When my daughter was in high school, one of her classmates passed away. It was a tough week for all the children, as they had to face death at an early age. On the day of the funeral, nearly the entire school showed up at the local skate park to celebrate the life of the young man. At the entrance to the skate park, an employee from a local business stood quietly. She was handing out single carnations to all the young kids. A short poem was attached to each flower. There was no mention of any brand or any commercialization. The brand was simply being present and being a good neighbor by bringing in some flowers for the person we'd lost. There was something humble about this gesture; there was something truly authentic. The store and its employee were part of the community based on their actions.

After a few days, I visited the restaurant, but not just because they were distributing carnations at the memorial service. Instead, I felt good about them being in the neighborhood and was appreciative of the way they were part of the local community and made me feel good about the brand. The restaurant truly did good karma that day. They did not think about what they would gain or how to get business out of those who had gathered; instead, they looked at what they could do to help the community heal.

Real Estate Agent Taking Care of Neighbors

Now let me talk to you about a business that is community based, run by a real estate agent who takes pride in being an expert in that community's real estate. Most real estate agents always try to be in a promotional mode. They distribute magnets, put ads in the community directory frequently, and send you postcards to share the news anytime they sell a home in the neighborhood. There is nothing wrong with all of the above, but can the agent go beyond the trinkets and truly contribute to the community? What if the real estate agent offered anyone in the community free vacation-care services, meaning that anytime anyone was going out of town, the agent would keep an eye on the house, pick up mail, water the plants, collect newspapers, and be there if anything else was required? These tasks are examples of help any good neighbor would offer. Over the years, the neighbors would feel connected to the agent, and that should result in the neighbors being loyal to their local real estate agent anytime they needed to buy or sell real estate.

In the dating example, as a comparison, consider how sensitive your date is. You watch how he talks to the servers carefully. When the lady at the next table drops something, he is the first to pick it up and give it to her. He is not a hero, but his natural, spontaneous actions touch your heart. He gets rewarded for the goodness of his heart, as his actions create a positive image in his date's mind.

In the same way, if a real estate agent calculates the amount of money he will make from selling a home, he will realize that free vacation-care services have a high return on investment (ROI). He is only putting in a few hours a week, and the potential reward for the good karma is in the thousands of dollars. The high rewards should incentivize him to find ways to offer the best free vacation-care services.

This example can be connected to three components of a brand's personality. They are

1. being true to one's self,
2. being caring and compassionate, and
3. having integrity.

I will talk in detail about integrity in the next section, but for now, let us blend these three traits together and conclude that brands that are good citizens are better choices for long-term relationships.

True Integrity

Those in the corporate world use the term *integrity* often, and an individual can be labeled as a person with high integrity. It is a defining label, as it creates a positive perception of the person. But what is integrity? Integrity does not have any legal definitions; it is not absolute. That being the case, how can brands define integrity? My grandma always told me, "Integrity is your internal compass. You use the compass to do the right thing when no one is around to judge you." This, to me, is an extension of the golden rule.

The relationship between integrity and trust is one of causality. When a brand acts with integrity, the brand is in a position to earn the trust of a customer. A customer's trust evolves over time, and that results in better customer relationships.

In the world of relationships, trust is earned over time when two people start counting on each other. Trust naturally grows over time and cannot be forced. A big driver of trust is the consistency of actions with little variability. When a person feels sure that he or she knows how his or her partner will react in a situation, that predictability results in consistency, and that consistency, over time, evolves into stronger trust. Consistency plays a critical role in a customer's relationship with a brand, as a brand earns trust when the customer has a consistent guest experience. A consistent guest experience comes when the guest gets the same level of high service over time, any time of the day, independent of which particular employee serves him or her, and in different locations for a multiunit retailer. Most brands have a gold standard of customer experience, and only when a brand takes a shortcut does the guest experience drop.

Ensuring no shortcuts is not a tactic; instead, it stems from a brand's integrity and how that principle permeates all levels of the organization.

Most of us grew up defining the term *integrity* as "doing the right thing when no one is watching." It is important to note that the right thing does not have any legal definition. Instead, it is subjective and is open to personal interpretation. My grandma took integrity a step further, as she defined it for me by saying, "As you are making any tough decision, always think I am standing by you and watching you carefully. Always make decisions that will give you no reason for regret later and make me proud." The thought of my grandma watching over me raised the bar of integrity for me.

Trusting You with My Pepperoni

Now, with this framework, let me go back to the pepperoni pizza example, in which a consultant advised that reduction of pepperoni would not be noticed by the guests but would result in millions of dollars in profit. If I were the consultant, this would be my effort to explain the cost-saving decision to my grandma, if she were standing next to me and watching me carefully: "Grandma, guess what! I have identified a unique way of helping my company make more profit than before. Currently, there are sixty pepperoni on the pizza. I have found that using thinner pepperoni and using only fifty-seven pepperoni will make the company an additional twelve million dollars a year. And what is most amazing, Grandma, is that the customers did not even taste the difference when I served the pizza with fewer pepperoni."

As I read what I just typed, I do not think this explanation would have gone well with my grandma. I imagine her being confused at first. She would have said, "Why will you give the customers less and charge them the same price to make more money? What would the customer think of the company if he or she realized that your company is giving him or her less pepperoni for the same money? What will the customer's feelings be when he or she realizes that your intent all along was to trick him or her by putting just enough pepperoni on the pizza so that he or she thinks the pizza is the same? Would you be able to go share directly with the customer the same story that you are sharing with me?" As I think of what my grandma would have said, I am not feeling proud of bringing the idea to her.

It is not illegal to offer fewer pepperoni on a pizza at the same price without disclosing it to customers, but is that the right thing to do? Doing the right thing is subject to personal interpretation, and a brand will open itself up to a lot of challenges if it lets every employee decide what the right thing to do is. If corporate comes up with a clever fewer-pepperoni pizza, why can individual stores not find other ways to reduce further toppings on the pizza? By rolling out the new pepperoni pizza as something the customer did not notice, isn't the brand setting a culture all through the company that encourages staff to take shortcuts as long as they do not get caught? That approach might take the company down a slippery slope of shortcuts, and customer experience is bound to drop over time. Only integrity with no shortcuts can result in a consistent customer experience over time, which in turn earns trust over time. In a relationship, if one lives by the principle "I am only going to do things that I will not get caught doing," it will lead the person down a slippery slope. The chances of a relationship blossoming after that will be small.

Making Fun of Others

I am originally from India, and although it might not be evident to you as you read this, I have an accent that is unique to me. Today my accent is a blend of what it was when I left India and my adaptions as I have communicated in this country. I am accepting of my accent and view it as a dimension of my communication and nothing else, but still, when someone mimics my accent or an Indian accent, I become uncomfortable. I do not jump up and protest. Instead, I assume a laughing-with-you approach and put on a forced smile. I have to admit that I do not like those moments. Usually, right after that, I cut short the conversation and I hide my discomfort by simply being present. In a way, I withdraw a big part of me from the conversation and barely stay engaged.

Insurance Spokesperson We Love

One of the recent successful advertisements for an insurance company features a young lady who goes out of the way to solve customer problems. She is smart and always on her toes and knows what to say to engage customers. She has broken through the clutter as a great brand spokesperson coming out of nowhere. Now, through this, the brand can launch quite a few different new products. In fact, she is an established bridge over which customer-centric messages are transmitted with a greater degree of communication effectiveness. This is brilliant marketing. Now imagine you work for the company. When you wake up in the morning and get dressed to go to work, how do the ads make you feel? When you interact with customers, do the ads set an expectation that you find hard to deliver? If both of your reactions are positive, then the ads did an excellent job of increasing team members' morale.

Making Fun of the Pizza Delivery Driver

The same holds true for team members. I have been on teams where together we created breakthrough advertising in which I added personality and attitude to the brand by not portraying team members in the most flattering way. If you add some clever camera angles, it is inevitable that the team member featured in the ad will stand out as nerdy, funny, or a little strange. I remember a particular pizza advertisement in which the customer sees the delivery driver through the peephole. The visual of the delivery driver is made more memorable with the use of the camera angle. In short, the driver is made to look somewhat dorky. If you were a delivery driver for that pizza company, what would you feel after that television advertisement came out? Would you be comfortable in a social setting when your friends ask you to make that face? How would you feel if, when delivering a pizza to a family, as the mom is getting ready to pay, the little girl announces, "Mommy, Mommy! Our delivery driver doesn't look funny like the guy on television. Can you please order from the funny guy next time?"

Quite a few brands want to portray their employees as nerdy and want to be funny in their advertising. However, the blend of nerdy and funny is not always flattering for the employees. Do brands pause and see what effect the advertising has on team members? When employees are on the job, do they get uncomfortable? Do they not like it but act politically correct, simply being on the job? I would even go a step beyond by asking if they are offended by being ridiculed. I did not take this issue seriously until a few years back. During a client off-site, the CEO of the company started talking to the entire team in an accent that was an attempt to resemble one of his direct reports. The imitation was not authentic enough to make the man feel flattered. Instead, the exaggerated imitation was more of mimicry and was aimed at amusing everyone on the senior management team. We all knew whom he was making fun of, and that person was not laughing with the group. That moment dampened his energy and enthusiasm. During the rest of the off-site, that team member became disengaged and did the minimum amount required of him. If the CEO had known this would happen, would he have mimicked him? Also, the rest of us were a little nervous, as each of us was worried that the CEO might mimic any one of us in a public forum. The CEO was simply trying to connect with all of us by being funny, but his insensitivity made the entire off-site less effective.

Let me now take this example to the dating world. During your date, you take a picture of your date from a strange angle that makes her nose look longer, and the camera is focused on the inside of her nose. I hope you delete the picture immediately. If you think it is funny and choose to either share it with friends or put it on social media, I am sure that your date will not find the attention a pleasant experience.

To internalize this, the next time you turn on your television and watch any ad featuring the team members of a company, think about how you would feel if you or a close family member worked for that company. Would you feel excited that you and the team were featured in the advertisement? Or would you feel weird? Would you get defensive and say, "Nope, I am not like that, and I do not like to be portrayed that way"? Then try to look at what specifically bothers you the most. Is it that the volume of the person speaking in the ad is somewhat loud? Is it that the wardrobe is kind of out of the ordinary? Or is it some strange mannerism? Usually, ads use a combination of these traits to grab the viewers' attention and help the brand break through the clutter.

Another area that commonly mocks individuals is comparative marketing. Making fun of employees working for competitive brands is looked at as fair game. It is even used to motivate a brand's team members. But do brands realize the following in the ever-changing working environment?

- In the past, a sizable percentage of a brand's current team members worked for the competition.
- As a brand continues to grow, it will tap the skilled and experienced workforce that is currently working for the competition.

Based on the above, brands should ask themselves, "Is the gain from making fun of team members (internal or competitive) worth it? Or should marketing look at other ways to have amusing, breakthrough advertising without making fun of team members?" I have to admit that quite a few advertisements that laugh at the team members are successful. To me, these kinds of advertisements are bad karma directed toward team members and usually do not result in good customer karma. I think the marketing gains more by showing team members in the proper light instead of making fun of them.

Good Karma Is Not for Sale

I believe that trying to buy good karma is the first step in taking the relationship for granted. As we have seen, the rewards of good karma in the business world can be significant. Brands can get desperate to get to the rewards of good karma. Some of the actions brands take in desperation include the following.

1. **Loyalty Is Not a Program:** Loyalty evolves over time; it is a natural evolutionary phase in a relationship. It is not a recipe-driven program.
2. **Outsourcing Love:** When you pay someone to do good karma on your behalf, then even if the karma is good, it does not have your fingerprints on it. As you did not actually do the good karma, is it fair for you to expect that good karma will come back to you? I do not think so, as payment makes it a transactional relationship, but good karma is not transactional.

3. **Discounting Love:** If instead of doing good karma, you try to pay your customer, should it result in good karma returning to you?
4. **Affection Disclaimers:** Affection is unconditional. Adding conditions to affection limits the relationship.

Loyalty Cannot Be Programmed

I have clearly stated that the goal of this journey is to create a stronger relationship with your customers. In the business world, the customer relationship is centered on the word *loyalty*. First, let me look a little deeper into the meaning of that word. *Oxford Dictionaries*[3] defines *loyalty* as "a strong feeling of support or allegiance." To me, it is a connection that is built by both parties and earned over time. When I apply that concept to business, I must acknowledge that the customers have the power, as they have choices. A business, through consistent, outstanding service, has to earn each customer's loyalty one customer at a time. If there were a measure of commitment, the measure would increase or decrease over time based on what each party put into the relationship. A business can measure its loyalty at any point in time but must understand that commitment tomorrow can increase or decrease based on how the business treats the customer today. To simplify, loyalty comes from the customer experiencing repeated good karma and starting to expect it from the business.

In business, one of the most common misuses of the word *loyalty* is when people use it to describe a loyalty program. Now, pause for a moment and think. For those of you who are in a long-term relationship, if you went to your significant other and said, "Honey, you will be so happy to know that I have launched a loyalty program for you," I don't have to define for you what his or her expression would be and how much you would regret saying this.

Loyalty Rewards for Your Date

Most businesses are investing heavily in loyalty programs. However, when you take a step back and try to break down the components of a typical loyalty program, you will see that most so-called loyalty programs are based on the following three elements.

1. First, they track the behavior of every customer. This is no less intrusive than stalking every customer. Brands often will access customers' buying behavior away from the store by getting their credit card purchase behavior.
2. Next, they identify every personal and behavioral detail of all the customers who are spending the most money with the business (these customers are called heavy users) or who have the potential to do so in the future (these are medium users).
3. Finally, they throw carrots at the medium users so that they can become heavy users, and they give the heavy users something as a reward so that they continue spending a considerable amount of money with the brand. The carrot, or incentive, in most cases is either a dollar amount off or free auxiliary product, which the customers would not have purchased on their own. This is simply an effort to buy customers' loyalty to move them up the loyalty ladder.

Based on the above components of a loyalty program, the essence of a loyalty program as it exists today can be described as stalking, monitoring, and, finally, buying love.

Now let me go back to the example of a loyalty program in personal life, which I intentionally did not finish. Let me pick up from the place where you told your significant other, "Honey, I have a loyalty program for you." It might sound ridiculous, but bear with me. Imagine you are a single man, you meet a person, and you like her. As both of you just met, you think she sees other people too. You do not like that. To make her loyal to you, you start tracking her actions and monitoring her behavior and her attitude toward you. Then you realize that she is going out with you once every two weeks. You invent an incredible reinforcement program. Every fifth time she goes out with you, you send her flowers. In fact, you tell her ahead of time, "Girl, every fifth time you go out with me, you will get the most beautiful flowers from me. It will be the best carnation bouquet you will ever see." Then you go on to say, "But that is just the beginning. Every third time you get flowers from me, I will upgrade the bouquet to roses." Then you pause to see her excitement at this offer.

Even though you know what her response to the program will be, for the sake of this example, let's assume she continues to play this game. Let's also assume she gets excited about this and starts seeing you more often. You love that and immediately apply the program.

Now that she sees you on a weekly basis, you want her to continue to do so, so every time you go out, you get her a free dessert. Nice, huh? And you continue to give her things to reward her and reinforce a higher level of loyalty. In life, if this is not the perfect way to build a relationship, I do not know what is! Okay, I am being sarcastic. If she has gone along with your plan, by now, she is sure to ask, "What is seriously wrong with this guy?"

We all know that this experiment in life might not work, even if you are the only man she can find. Even then, it will become a real transactional connection. Yes, she will be loyal to you, and there will be some Pavlovian influence on her behavior that gets reinforced by your incentives, but is that the best way to build a lasting relationship?

A brand must revisit the concept of customer karma over and over to realize that the ultimate reward for doing good karma to a customer is to earn the customer's trust and loyalty. It needs to offer sincere one-on-one attention during every interaction with the customer. The brand must be full of self-belief and confidence, as the customer is bound to reward good karma in due time.

Outsourcing Love

Why does a brand not immerse itself in winning the heart of a customer? Why does it not follow Julia Roberts's line from the movie *Pretty Woman*:[4] "I will treat you so nice that at the end of the week, you will not let me go"?

The reason this does not happen today is simply because loyalty programs are in the wrong hands. Who is face-to-face with the customers? A team member who is serving the customers. And who is in charge of the loyalty program? Marketing employees who are sitting at corporate headquarters. Even worse, the company outsources the development of the loyalty program to a loyalty vendor, who will stalk, monitor, and buy love to increase loyalty. Marketing going to a third party to find ways to strengthen the relationship with customers is comparable to your coworker or assistant sending flowers to your girlfriend on her birthday on your behalf. Shouldn't you be the one who chooses the perfect gift? In the same way, shouldn't front-line team members, who interact with customers, be in charge of building relationships with the customers?

An Open Letter of Disclosure to the Customer

Now let me talk about the outsourcing part of this arrangement. Over time, companies feel that they have successfully outsourced customer loyalty to the hands of the outside vendor and start focusing on the process of serving customers. The heart and passion in the guest connections erode. The outsourcing might sound efficient, as now team members can focus on the task of delivering the service to customers. If a company chooses to disclose to its customers what a loyalty vendor is doing for them, then the disclosure will read like this:

Dear Customer,

We are excited to share with you that we have partnered with a loyalty vendor to assist us. This company is an outside company and is not part of our organization. They will monitor what you buy, when you buy, with whom you are coming to our store, and how much you spend. We want to inform you that we will track the credit cards you use with us and, with the help of the credit card company, try to study what else you buy using the credit cards. But all this is to serve you better. We will study other customers who have similar buying behavior and determine what kind of offers will get you to come to us more often and spend more money. We have engaged this expert outside our organization so that you and our company can have a closer relationship.

After I wrote this disclosure, I read it a few times, and every time, it scared me to see how far brands are going to get more business. I also wonder where customers will go five to ten years from now.

The picture becomes clearer if you translate this to a relationship. Imagine a person in a long-term relationship finds a custom outsourcing service. The outsourcing service offers to research and send the right gifts to his partner for Valentine's Day, her birthday, and Christmas. If ever he has challenges in the relationship, all he has to do is inform them of the problem. They will go through their database and identify what the best solution in similar circumstances has been, and they will implement it on his behalf. Unlike the business example, in this case, the outsourcing does not come across as better for the relationship. In fact, in this case, the person's heart is no longer present in the relationship, and without one's heart involved, there will be an emotional void in the connection. In the same way, outsourcing loyalty programs prevents the team members from engaging with their hearts in serving customers.

A Folk Song from Bengal

In India, I come from the state of West Bengal. In my mother tongue, Bengali, there is a folk song[5] that, when translated, goes like this: "If you write a name on a piece of paper, it can tear. If you write your name on a rock, that too can erode over time. But if you write your name on a heart, that will stay forever." Isn't that the way a relationship should be built with customers, one customer at a time?

One of the best ideas a brand can have for building a stronger relationship with its customers is to empower its team members to wow them one customer at a time. Team members know how to treat their best friend; empowering them is all it will take. No one else from the company should be in the way. They should only be there to help team members celebrate their success.

I have nothing against companies that sell loyalty programs. Such companies justify their existence by claiming that they are specialists and that their method is more effective and efficient than traditional ways of marketing. Of course, they are right, as they have the numbers to prove their effectiveness. Often, businesses find it convenient to get into the habit of ongoing spending on maintaining loyalty. This is the equivalent of you paying a third party to manage your relationship with your significant other. If you are totally incapable of building a relationship, this third-party management still won't work.

Now let me take a step back and look at the bigger picture in life. In life, can you drive loyalty? Or is loyalty just a result of two people choosing to be in a relationship and earning loyalty over time? I think that the choice to be in a relationship comes first, and then trust builds over time, which leads to loyalty—and not the other way round. Hence, just using loyalty as a program to get into a stronger relationship with customers is a big whoa. If you have to use incentives to make a customer come back to you, you must realize that true love is missing from the connection, and that relationship might not last long.

Loyalty programs are not doing anything illegal, and outsourcing loyalty programs is not illegal. But let me show you why, in most cases, these programs don't work. Look at the trade area of a brand that breaks in the following way:

- Group 1: Those who are not aware of the brand — 20%
- Group 2: Those who are aware of the brand but have not tried it — 20%
- Group 3: Lapsed customers — 30%
  (Those who have not visited in the last six months)
- Group 4: Current customers — 20%
  (Those who have visited in the last six months but not in the last month)
- Group 5: Regular customers — 10%
  (Those who have visited in the last month)

A typical loyalty program gathers information from the stores and incentivizes customers to join the program. That means the loyalty program only gets members from group 5, some from group 4, and a few from group 3. The program has no way of getting members from groups 1 and 2. Real business growth will happen when a program can source from groups 1, 2, and 3. The loyalty program cannot do it, as it sources from those who are already coming to the store.

Offering discounts to this group has a high risk of cannibalizing the brand. What is wrong with cannibalizing? If a customer buys a product at a discounted price, after that, the customer might not come back and pay full price. I believe that groups 1 and 2 need a wow-inducing guest experience in which the employees connect with customers' hearts to increase the emotional connection to the brand. Discount-offer-based loyalty programs simply try to give a rational reason to the customer to come more often.

If a company to whom you have outsourced the program is deciding what type of loyalty program to implement, they will go by the numbers. But if your company team members are deciding on this, they need to put in perspective the potential long-term relationship with the customer. Hence, outsourcing a relationship management system might not build a relationship with the customer.

Discounting Love

I want to meet the person who invented coupons. What was his or her thought process when inventing them? I feel that coupons are value-gap correctors, as they are a brand's way of covering up the shortcoming of its offering.

The Best Haircut Ever

A new brand that is launching men's haircuts for twenty-five dollars just entered the marketplace. This deal is being marketed as the best thing that ever happened to haircuts. Team members start by taking a picture of the customer and showing him digitally how he would look with different haircut options. After the customer chooses a style, a team member prints an image and places it in front of the customer as the haircut starts. The hairstylist acts as an artist, trimming the hair and delivering a cut that is guaranteed to look like the promised picture.

Now, let me share how the marketing team can use coupons to promote this new product. First, they might come up with an introductory offer for new customers to try the new haircut for fifteen dollars. To the brand, it might make sense to get customers to try the new haircut at a reduced price. The company can easily justify the ten-dollar acquisition cost by looking at the lifetime value of customers. This strategy might even pay off after the second visit. Let me assume that at the end of the first week, each haircut studio was buzzing with new customers, and the coupon created a high level of awareness. Before I call this coupon a brilliant move by marketing, let me review this offer from the store operators' point of view. Each store hired a bunch of new hairstylists to meet the increase in demand. Even though the hairstylists might have been trained well, they are new to the job. Instead of slowly getting used to this new job, from day one, they are forced to have a full schedule and work in a high-stress situation to perform at the high standard promised by the store. The business model hinges on the assumption that a happy customer will spread positive word of mouth and be excited to return and pay full price, which is ten dollars more, for the next haircut. Getting the customer to pay ten dollars more for the next visit is no easy task, as the customer paid only fifteen dollars for the first cut. In order for that to happen, during the experience, the customer needs to feel so wowed by the experience that he insists on paying more the next time. Of course, marketing will try to justify this by saying that the customer realizes that this is a twenty-five-dollar haircut and that the fifteen-dollar price is a great value for a low-risk trial. But did marketing take the easy road by offering a discount and putting the onus on employees to deliver the value? Should marketing have instead stepped up and communicated the new breakthrough haircut, the best haircut a man ever had? Product development came up with a fabulous new product; store employees were all geared up to deliver a superior experience. In that context, shouldn't marketing have taken up the challenge of effectively communicating the message "Get a haircut like never before" instead of buying visits at a discount?

Using a Coupon for Free Dessert to Get a Date

In the dating world, this concept would be the equivalent of someone placing the following adverisement on a dating site: "Here is a coupon for a free dessert! If you respond to my post and go out with me, within the next two weeks, I will buy you a free dessert. Just know that it is my guarantee that this will be the best offer you will receive from anyone on the site. If someone else makes a better offer, I promise to match it. So when can we go out?" Now, if that is not a clear example of bad karma, I do not know what is. If this type of tactic is clearly bad karma, then why do businesses rely so heavily on coupons?

Desperate Efforts to Try to Make a Guest Come Back

Let's look at another coupon. This one is called a comeback coupon. Before a customer leaves, the hairstylist hands the customer a coupon that says, "If you come back in the next thirty days, you can get your next haircut at ten dollars off." There is a logical justification for this. I have learned that new customers need to try a new product at least two to three times before they become loyal users of the brand. But how does the hairstylist feel giving out the coupon? Is he or she conceding that he or she did not provide the high level of service he or she was aiming for? Is he or she acknowledging that the service he or she provided was only a fifteen-dollar service, or is he or she revealing he or she is unsure of the value offered by providing the coupon? The hairstylist is getting used as a marketing delivery vehicle for the coupon to ensure customer retention. Let's go back to the friend example from the previous chapter. Would you ever consider giving your friend a coupon for ten dollars off a haircut as a birthday gift? Of course not. Then why is the hairstylist being used to deliver the coupon?

Please do not get me wrong, as I believe that brands need to find ways to generate trial and give customers reasons to come back. But as a brand develops these plans, it must have a clear idea of the following.

- What is the price of your product? From day one, you need to make sure the customer is familiar with the price and is comfortable paying that amount for the product long term.
- If you are educating the customer that a ten-dollar-off coupon is an excellent reason to try your product, are you not opening the door for a desperate competitor to compete with you on price? You know that starting an intense price war hurts all competitors and is tough to exit.
- If you want to generate trial, why not send invites for a free haircut to some of the opinion leaders in the community? If this offer is made selectively, it will generate trial yet not get all new customers to try the brand at a discounted price.

If I compare this approach to a dating situation, it translates into a man offering his date a coupon that says, "If you go out with me again in the next thirty days, I will throw in a free dessert on our next date." In doing so, the man shows his insecurity, and that might make his date hesitant to go out with him again in the future.

I feel a more positive finish to the experience would have been to have a more enthusiastic reaction from the hairstylist: "Look at the picture, and look at yourself now. You chose a cut that perfectly suits you. I am digitally saving this on our system in your account; you can have access to it at any of our locations around the city. Going forward, unless you want to change your hairstyle, this will be the same consistent look for you. I recommend booking an appointment with me in three weeks. Of course, I will be flattered if you request me when you book your next appointment." Instead of giving the hairstylist the job of delivering a comeback coupon, empowering him or her to carry on a conversation might have been a better relationship builder for the brand.

Affection Disclaimers

Now that I have examined the true meaning of coupons and how they impact employees, let me take a closer look at all the fine print on a coupon. Coupons have legal disclaimers, expiration dates, and other restrictions of use. I am not here to argue the legal disclaimers and other restrictions but to ask you a simple question: When you give your date something, do you add a fine-print disclaimer?

Disclaimer for a Date

Let's go back to the dating example. Let me share with you an example of a hypothetical personal ad placed on a leading dating site. The advertiser created more urgency by changing the blurb to the following: "Here are a few reasons for you to go out with me. Here is a coupon for a free dessert. Please note it is not valid for weekends, but it's a great offer if we go out on a weeknight. If we go out on a weekend, I will get you a ten-dollar-off coupon for your next fifty dollars spent at a leading cosmetics store. If you commit to two dates, I will pay for your entrée on our second date. I call it my special POGO offer, where you pay for one dinner and get the second one free. Are you excited? When can we go out?" I cannot think of a single person putting any offers like this on a dating site. Thus, I have to ask: If you would never consider any of the above offers to get your next date, why would you consider them to get your next customer? Shouldn't you be consistent in both relationships, your dating and your customer acquisition?

Weekday-Only Offer (Means Not Good during Weekends)

As you are still thinking about that unique post on a dating site, are you wondering why some retailers and restaurants put on their coupons "Valid at participating locations only"? It is a glass-half-full way of saying, "Some locations might not take this coupon, but go ahead and try your luck." Sometimes coupons say, "Valid for the next two weeks only." I find this limitation to be somewhat manipulative and trying too hard to get the customer to return in the next two weeks. If a brand is so desperate to get the customer to return in the next two weeks, why not tempt the customer with exciting news about something that will happen in the next two weeks? That way, the customer will leave the store already thinking of why he or she has to return in the next two weeks.

In the dating experience, this coupon approach would be similar to a man asking his date out with a note that says the following: "I would like to go out but not to all restaurants. Give me the names of restaurants, and I will tell you if we can go there or not." The time-validity part would translate to "If we go out in the next two weeks, I will pay for one alcoholic beverage." This offer translates in the dating world as "I would feel insecure in our relationship if you did not go out with me in the next two weeks."

Coupon Therapy

When I focus on the business aspect and analyze these coupons, the following three questions come to mind.

1. **Why do marketers of multiunit businesses want to promote an offer that is not accepted in all units?** Is there a rule that at least 50 percent of stores have to accept the offer for you to legally make the offer, or can you make the offer if even one store accepts the offer? We might perceive the offer as deceptive advertising. Marketers think customers will like the offer in general and visit the store. When a customer goes to the wrong store and the store does not accept the coupon, he or she is bound to be disappointed. This is the equivalent of you warning your date you will be nice to her only on certain days. You do not share with her the list of days, and she has to take a chance by going out on a date with you and finding out if that is a day you have chosen to be nice to her.

2. **What does disappointment do to the customer?** At the very least, it irritates the customer, but it can also make customers extremely upset. They might feel tricked. Even though customers might still buy something because they are in the store, their trust in the brand starts to erode, and that trust is a pillar of customer loyalty. Since a big part of any relationship is based on emotional connection, breaking a customer's trust is similar to having a major setback in a dating relationship. I am not saying that a major setback in a dating relationship will break the relationship completely, but it will take a lot of effort to recover from.
3. **What position does this limited offer put the employee in?** It forces the operations employee to say no in stores that do not accept the offer. Employees have no chance to succeed and wow the customer when they are put in a situation where they cannot say yes. An interaction between an employee who is embarrassed by saying no to the customer and a customer who is upset is not the recipe for building a brand.

These kinds of marketing offers pop up everywhere. Consider these situations.

- Let me start with the famous BOGO offer. *BOGO* stands for "buy one and get one" free. If a customer fails to read the fine print, he or she might realize only after coming to the store that instead of getting two for the price of one, he or she gets a coupon for a free product the next time he or she is in the store.
- Sometimes an offer is only valid for specific times of the day or week. This kind of offer is limiting, and usually, the specified times favor the brand and not the customer. Effectively, the brand is saying, "Here is a list of times our business is down. If you come during those times, we will reward you."
- According to some offers, to receive the discount advertised, the customer needs to pay full price and then get a store credit or a coupon in the mail. This offer creates uncertainty because of the delayed gratification. Does the customer perceive the delayed

gratification to be less of a value than an immediate gratification? In the dating world, a comparable example would be a man telling his date, "Instead of bringing you flowers, I have made arrangements to send flowers to your home after our date. Getting the flowers is simple. Just go online, and put this specific information on the site. Then flowers should get to you in the next four to six days." I am not sure if any good karma would come to him for gifting these flowers.

Marketers must take on the responsibility of setting expectations that can be fulfilled. Some time back, a major ladies' purse manufacturer ran a print ad featuring a celebrity. The advertisement generated a lot of interest, but there was one problem: the bag featured in the ad had been out of production for the last six years. The ad was successful, and it got customers to the store to purchase the bag. But what happened next? The store employees had to explain that the specific bag was unavailable and was not in production at all. This event resulted in a huge number of disappointed customers. Customers had to settle for the second-best purse choice or for something they did not seek.

My request to all marketers reading this is the following: Please do not make things difficult for store employees by setting expectations that are too high or making offers that are limiting. Store employees have a tough job of fulfilling customers one at a time. Please do not make their task tougher by forcing them have to say no at the beginning of a customer experience. It is similar to a first date starting with a disappointing moment.

If marketing chooses to ignore the above request and still sends out offers that are conditional and limiting, is there anything a team member can do to save the experience? Of course, the team member can always ignore the fine print and accept the coupon with a smile. This way, the experience does not have to start with the team member saying no.

Showing Love with Just a Hot Towel

I have talked about what a brand should not do. Now let's look at an example of what a brand can do to truly touch a customer's heart. The effort from the brand has to be sincere and authentic. I want to share a recent example that took me by surprise.

A Hot Towel Is All It Took to Wow

For the last three to four years, I have been going to the same haircut place. My routine is the same: I get the same haircut and then get a shampoo. During the shampoo, the stylist puts a hot towel on my face. The haircut place has my preference recorded, and any location I go to can access my preference and ensure that I get the same experience. They have become the epitome of consistency by delivering the same experience without fail over time, from store to store and stylist to stylist. However, on a recent visit, things changed.

As the stylist was leading me to the shampoo room after my haircut, she said, "Mr. Sen, I see that you have been coming to us for the last four years. Since you come every month, it is evident that you do not go anywhere else for your haircut. We truly appreciate you trusting us with this responsibility. We want to thank you for your patronage by offering you a free second hot-towel treatment." I said thank you, even though I was not sure what she meant. As I sat down to get my hair shampooed, she put a hot towel on my face. After a minute, she removed it and then put a second hot towel on my face. Wow, that was special. I am not being sarcastic. I looked at other customers, and no one else was getting the second towel. I was excited like a little kid. When the shampoo was over, I thanked her again for the second hot towel, but this time, my words were full of enthusiasm and energy. I specifically thanked her for the second hot towel. She smiled at me and told me, "Please get used to it, Mr. Sen, as you will get it every time from now on." This was unbelievable.

Within three weeks, I was back for my next haircut. Normally, I get my hair cut every four weeks, but the anticipation of the second hot towel got me to the store a week early. I have to be honest that a part of me was worried that the little kid in me would be disappointed, as the store might have forgotten the promise about the second hot towel. But I was hopeful. The store did not let me down. As I was sitting down for shampooing, the stylist removed the first towel and put the second one on me, and I could not stop myself from spontaneously saying, "Yesss." That second hot towel completely changed my connection with the brand; it brought magic back into the relationship.

As I thought about this over and over, I realized the brand must have a process in place to deliver consistent service. Every employee was sold on the process and had no intention of taking any shortcuts. Without the process and the commitment from the employees, the brand would not have been able to make the promise "You will get it every time from now on" and deliver on it. They also chose to give me something relevant that others did not get, and the bonus happened toward the end of the experience. All of this ensured that I left the store with a big smile and could not wait to come back for the next haircut. The offer of a second hot towel forever hit me emotionally. This ongoing offer feels like being in a long hug with a person you love, and just when you are done with the hug, she pulls you close and holds you tightly. That spontaneous action shows affection and takes the connection to a deeper level that can be felt but not explained.

The proof of success for the idea was how I reacted. That said, brands need to find ways to bring occasional magic back into the relationship. Otherwise, the brand becomes too predictable and might turn out to be a little boring over time. I wanted to finish this section with this example to show that actions that touch the heart do not have to come from complicated programs or big offers. Simple actions delivered with sincerity can go a long way toward connecting with the customer and building a strong long-term relationship.

Be Focused and Add a Personal Touch

When you do good karma to someone, what touches the other person is your sincerity and effort. The deed starts with focus, when you take time to figure out what a person likes and act to deliver that. Imagine you buy a cool gift for a coworker of yours. He is excited about your kind, thoughtful gesture. However, the next morning at work, when he realizes that you have given everyone at work the same gift, he does not feel special anymore. He wanted to be the only one; he wanted you to treat him differently and put in a personal touch for him that no one else got.

One can achieve this personal touch through the following.

1. **Maintain a Commitment to Focus:** Focus is essential for a brand if it wants to build a relationship. Being the same brand consistently over time gives the customer a chance to know the brand and start trusting it.
2. **Recognize What Not to Focus On**: The power of focus helps a brand clearly determine what not to work on.

Once that clarity is shared with the entire organization, a brand can maximize its power to serve the customer.

3. **Love through One-on-One Connection**: Pausing for a customer and making the customer feel one-of-one love results in the customer realizing that he or she is important to the brand.

Curly's One Thing

Let me go back to story of the seven blind men and the elephant, in which each man looks only at a part of the elephant to decipher what it is. After figuring out that the object in front of them is an elephant, they are given the task of building a room for the elephant. As they start their task together, they must focus on the elephant, the big picture, and the overall goal of creating the structure for the elephant. If each blind man only focuses on the part of the elephant he experienced, the limited focus will not lead them to a successful completion of the task. I am sure that the solution they would come up with based on seeing the elephant only as a rope or a pillar would not be a room that would fit the elephant.

A Juggling CEO

Translating this example to the business world, a company must focus on what the customers' needs are and how to fulfill them in the long term. A big part of the focus is to determine what not to work on and what one does best. Here is a favorite example of mine. The CEO of a company arrived at an annual planning session with six different-colored juggling balls. He clumsily tried to juggle the balls without much success. He was stubborn and continued but did not succeed. Then he dropped the orange ball and moved to a five-ball juggling trick. That too was not working. Then he dropped the brown ball. Now he was down to four. He did much better with four balls, but when he dropped the white ball and only had the red, yellow, and blue balls to juggle, he was perfect. Of course, all of us stood up and clapped at the performance. The CEO stopped, caught all three balls, and took a bow. Then he looked at all of us and said, "Guys, times are tough, and the companies that will survive will have to focus on what we work on. We should not even try to juggle all six balls at the same time. Let us change the game to a three-ball juggling act. The three the three initiatives that will take us to success. Now, let hoose which three balls we must use, keeping in mind our eeds." Just when the rest of us in the room were getting ready to start our juggling practice, the CEO directed our attention to the red ball. He said, "Team, this is the ball that matters. This ball symbolizes the customer. However good a juggler you are, if you drop this ball, the game is over."

A Golf Tee Shot over Water

The power of focusing is relevant in every field, especially sports. As I was working on a branding project with one of the top golfers in the world, he enlightened me by saying, "At any time, if you can identify the one thing you must focus on and ignore the rest, that is the best recipe for success. I play one golf round at a time, I play one hole at a time, I play one shot at a time, and I also focus on one target at a time. In fact, when I am going to get ready for the drive on this hole, I will concentrate on that tree on the right. I will adjust my focus then on the right branch that is sticking out. Once I have that clarity of target, my only thought is to set the ball on a journey to that target." The same day, as we were playing a round of golf, we came to a par three with an island green. Before my tee shot, he asked me, "So what is your focus on this hole?" I smiled and said my focus on that hole would be not to get the ball in the water. He laughed and said, "Do you know the first word we all learn to ignore in life? It is the word *no*. We hear it so often that we develop some immunity to the word. So when you said that your focus on this hole will be not getting the ball in the water, your mind dropped the word *not*. Hence, your mind locked in your focus as getting the ball in the water, and once you are that focused on a target that big in front of you, guess where you will be sending the ball. The water." This was a big learning moment for me, though I use this knowledge more off the golf course, as I still regularly hit the ball into the water on a hole with water. However, in the corporate world, I learned that the focus has to be on something positive, something clear. Focus cannot be clarity on what I do not want to focus on. That is too complicated.

In the same way, if your date calls you and nervously shares that she is kind of lost while driving, the only thing you need to focus on at that moment is how to guide her. You should pause everything else in life, as only after that can you focus on helping. If she is rattled by getting lost, maybe you can think of guiding her to the nearest gas station and take a cab to the gas station. Once you are there, she will be happy and relieved to see you. It does not matter how many times you have told her that you love her; in that moment, she will be overflowing with emotion and appreciation that you dropped everything to come rescue her. Your being physically there will be the emotional connection, and your dropping everything and taking care of her will be the rational justification that will strengthen the emotional connection.

Curly Speaking

By now, you likely have figured out that I find inspiration from movie classics. Every time I need clarity on focus, I go back to Curly's words in the movie *City Slickers*.[6]

> Curly: Do you know what the secret of life is? [He holds up one finger.] This.
> Mitch: Your finger?
> Curly: One thing. Just one thing. You stick to that, and the rest don't mean shit.
> Mitch: But what is the one thing?
> Curly: [He smiles.] That's what you have to find out.

In the corporate world, it is easy to get distracted by the challenges of the day and forget the customer. Any time I lost my focus, I would immediately remind myself of Curly's character holding up one finger or the CEO holding up that red ball. Both of these powerful visuals are reminders of the power of focus. But there is a challenge. No one can deny the importance of focus, nor does anyone argue with the rewards one can get because of focus, but the question is this: How do you focus? Here are two steps I have found that help with focus.

Step 1: Clearly define what the purpose is. This is essential, as without this step, brands often focus their attention on what is convenient for them to focus on. An example is when a brand starts by choosing to focus its media dollars on social media. Before a brand can successfully develop a social media strategy, shouldn't the brand do the following?

- Have a clear idea of who its customer is.
- Identify what message to get through to the customer.

Only then should a brand get into the media choice. Hence, focusing alone does not work; focusing on the right thing is essential.

Step 2: Choose what not to work on. Once a brand identifies what to focus on, it must have the discipline to implement it. Implementation starts by identifying what not to focus on. An example of this is relevant in the local marketing plan for retail brands. Once the brand decides on its focus direction, it then must decide not to put any resources on any other initiatives, however attractive the opportunities might be. This discipline allows a brand to stay true to its focus.

These two steps above are essential in order for brands to implement focus and realize the rewards.

Will Never Hit a 5-Iron Hybrid from a Fairway Bunker (Again)

No one will argue the importance of focus, but the challenge is how to drop everything when a situation arises. This has always been a challenge for me, but I found my answer when I was golfing with a top-ranked golf player.

Stuck in a Sand Bunker

My drive hit the edge of a fairway bunker and trickled back in. Once I went to the ball, I realized that I was 180 yards from the green. I grabbed my trusted hybrid equivalent of a 5-iron, choked down on it, and walked into the trap. I looked at the green, looked at the ball, and swung the club. I made good contact, and the ball left the club with high speed. However, it did not get out of the bunker and instead got buried on the front side of the bunker. Now I had an impossible shot. It took me two more shots to get out of the bunker and then an additional shot to the green, and I two putted. As I recorded a triple bogey on the scorecard, the golf professional asked me, "What happened there?"

I said, "I should not have used the hybrid equivalent of a five-iron; in fact, I should not have even used a six-iron. I should have used no more than a seven-iron to get simply out of the bunker."

The golf player paused and then asked, "Then why did you use the five hybrid?" I was not sure how to answer that. He then explained to me, "If you make a decision now that going forward, when you are in a fairway bunker, you will not use anything more than a seven-iron, it will be easy for you. The next time you are in a fairway bunker, the decision is made for you. But if it is a flat bunker and you have a great lie, you can then make the decision to use the five hybrid, but your default decision should be nothing more than a seven-iron."

I got it. I learned that if I knew what situations deserved priority attention, I could quickly turn everything off when any of those situations arose. I also learned that the journey to focus starts with defining what to take one's attention off of. This has improved my golf game and helped me get better at identifying the one thing I should be doing at any point in time in my professional and personal life. An immediate next step was changing the ringtone on my phone for my daughter's calls and making sure she was on the list of callers who could always get through to me. Since doing that, life has become easy, as anytime I hear that distinctive ringtone, I automatically excuse myself and take the call.

I touched on this idea briefly as one of the two action steps in the previous chapter, but how does it help in the business world? For that, I have to go back to my golf example. When I was trying to internalize the decision, the golf professional explained to me, "When you are in the bunker, you are looking at the world from the bunker. That is a totally different perspective from the one you had before the game. Hence, if you decide on what to focus on before you start the game, it is an easier decision."

In the same way, if a brand decides ahead of time what not to focus on, when it faces business decisions, it can easily pass on opportunities that would take way from its focus. Deciding on a focus earlier makes it an easy, efficient decision.

One of One and Not One of Many

In relationships or in business, if one does not pause to put his or her entire attention on a person, it is easy for the person to think that the other does not care enough for him or her.

Dating by the Numbers

Think of an imaginary friend of yours who thinks dating is a game of numbers. He believes that one has to date enough people to find the right person finally. He is serious about this strategy, in which he seeks one in many, but in the process, he targets as many dates as possible. He prides himself on sending fifty to sixty e-mails out to new prospective dates in an hour. I wonder how those on the receiving end of his dating numbers game take this. If you received one of his e-mails, wouldn't you find some disconnect in that e-mail? Wouldn't you feel that his perfect e-mail came from a factory and did not have the one-of-a-kind imperfection that would have touched you?

In my friend's case, the numbers game is a game of choice. But in the business world, many times, situations that become a numbers game are forced upon a team member. To understand this concept, look at the typical drive-through at a fast-food place. On a given day, an employee managing a drive-through might serve as many as sixty customers an hour. During that kind of frenzy, the employee might choose an overall goal to drive him or her: "How have I effectively served sixty customers in one hour?" To do this, the employee has to pay attention to multiple customers at the same time. Right after taking the order from a customer, as the employee starts to get the customer's food items, he or she multitasks by taking the order of the customer in the next car. As the first customer comes to the pickup window, ready to pay, he or she hears the employee repeat a different order. At that point, he or she realizes the employee is working with the next customer as he or she gets his or her order. He or she does not feel special anymore.

Day after Christmas at a Department Store

Let me share another example with you. Think of a couple of customer service personnel at a department store the day after Christmas, the biggest return day in the retail world. In this case, the employees are well trained and thoroughly committed to their task at hand.

As both of them look at the customer in front of them, they cannot stop looking at the huge line of customers behind this customer. Seeing the number of people, the employees put a lot of pressure on themselves. They try to hurry and be efficient, and they try to take care of the customer in front of them quickly so that they can get to the next person fast.

Now think from the point of view of the customers in each of the two lines. For example, a dad has come in first thing on the day after Christmas to exchange the leather jacket he bought for his beloved wife. He felt sad on Christmas morning when the jacket was slightly too big. He came into the store early and wants to get home with the right-sized jacket for his wife. I am going into details about this customer, as this trip to the department store has a lot of emotions connected to it. When he finally gets to the customer support person, he is somewhat anxious. He wants assurance that this time, he will get the right jacket and surprise his wife. He wants the employee to listen to him and provide him with all the help he needs.

Instead, the efficient employee greets him, takes the jacket and the receipt, and says, "Good. You have the receipt. I will hold on to this. Go get what you want, and come right back here." Before the man can say anything, the employee looks at the next customer in the line and says, "Next, please."

The man in search of the perfect jacket for his wife slowly heads to the women's department to choose a new jacket, but he feels something is missing. The employee was not rude; the employee was helpful, but still, the interaction left him wanting more. This is a vital moment for him, getting the exchange right is critical to him. He only wanted the employee to pause a little and spend more time with him. He wanted the employee to go online and help him find some information on how jacket sizes work for women. Instead of the employee finishing by saying, "Next," he wanted to hear from the employee, "Please go look and see if you find what you are looking for. If you cannot find what you are looking for, please come back, and I will find the clothing department manager to assist you. Please excuse us, as we are busy today, so it may take a few extra minutes' wait, but I can assure you that you will leave the store with the perfect jacket for your wife."

In both examples, the employee did not do anything wrong based on the employee user manual. The two employees merely saw the many customers and tried their best to distribute their attention equally to all people in line. In trying to make everyone's line shorter, they failed to acknowledge the customer in front and put all the attention only on the customer as long as he was in front of him or her. Good karma comes when an employee sees a customer as one of one, meaning that when serving the customer, the employee only focuses on him or her and nothing else. Giving one-of-many attention might be a more efficient process, but it does not get that level of good karma back to the business.

To me, here is an everyday business conflict. The employee is in serving-one-of-many mode, but each customer is out to get a one-on-one experience. A one-on-one experience means that the customer will only have, for example, one drive-through experience that day and wants it to be perfect. His or her expectations of one-on-one service are in conflict with the employees' one-of-many service plan. This emotion of the customer has been effectively shared in the following quote:

> Never allow someone to be your priority while allowing yourself to be their option.
> —Mark Twain

The customer has made the store his or her priority and chose it over all other options. The employee, on the other hand, has made the customer one of his or her options as he strives to serve all the customers at the same time. All the employee needs to do is pause for the customer in front of him or her and smile at him or her. That pause will break the rushed mind-set and connect with the customer by making him or her feel he or she is the employee's priority.

The employee pausing for the customer is a must for any buzzword or customer service plan to be effective. Only then can the customer feel good about the employee caring about only him or her at that instant. That is true one-on-one love.

Surviving Challenges

A relationship faces its true challenge when difficult times hit the relationship.

A Riddle from My Grandma

I want to share another piece of wisdom from my grandma in this context. This wisdom was more related to friendship than romance, but it can be applied to relationships as well. My grandma's story goes as follows. A long time ago, there were two friends. They were the best of friends as they grew up together. One day they went fishing and had to cross a fast-flowing river. There was a narrow bridge over the river, and without the bridge, it was impossible to cross the river. As they were returning, they heard a voice in the sky say, "Only one pair of feet can cross the bridge now. The bridge will be destroyed immediately after the first pair of feet crosses the bridge." When the friends heard the voice, each realized that only one of them would be able to go back to the other side. As they faced the ordeal, a real test of their friendship emerged. Who should cross the bridge first?

My grandma stopped her story there, and I wanted to know what happened at the end. "Did one of them run across first and save himself, Grandma? Or did one of them force his friend to go first and sacrifice his life?" I did not like stories without endings.

Finally, after a lot of nagging from me, Grandma went on to finish. "Think for a second. The difficult choice should have made the friends think together about how to overcome the challenge. As only one pair of legs could cross, why could they not cross the bridge with one carrying the other? Shouldn't that be how friendships work?" Grandma's example was brilliant, and the message made sense: there are no individuals in friendships and relationships.

Most customer challenges come when there is a perceived conflict of interest between a brand and a customer. However, if a brand thinks of a solution that puts the customer first, then both can win. Even though the customer might win in the immediate short term, the brand wins if the customer continues to have a long-term relationship with the brand. But if a brand is shortsighted and focuses only on the short term, it might miss the opportunity to survive the challenge and build a stronger, longer-lasting connection.

Let me share a few examples and evaluate how brands can act in each of the situations.

A takeout customer calls in and informs the restaurant that they made a mistake in his order. The restaurant employee says sorry and offers five dollars off the next time.

The customer did not call in for cash back. The customer called to share his frustrations, as he will only order one meal that evening, and the restaurant messed it up. The restaurant employee should understand that the customer might be far from the restaurant and might have been counting on the restaurant as the only option for his or his family's dinner that day. Hence, this error is significantly more severe than a dine-in customer's order not being right. For a dine-in customer, the restaurant could fix the mistake with a new order then and there. Understanding the seriousness, the employee should first express his or her apologies to the customer and then ask what, if anything, the restaurant can do to fix this mistake. "If you can drive down, we will have the right order ready for you. We want to throw in a free dessert for you too." The employee should offer free food for the future only at the end and not at the beginning.

A customer comes to a golf course on a busy Sunday morning and claims that he booked tee times for a foursome. The registration person takes all the details from the customer and checks the system. He then states that he cannot find any canceled or dropped reservations in the system at all. The course is booked that morning, but if the customer can be a little patient, the employee promises he will try to squeeze them in during the next hour.

I think if the customer is not right, there is no reason for the store to take the blame. That does not mean the store should confront the customer either. The registration person clearly expressed the policy and expressed his assurance that he would do everything he could to get the players teeing off in the next hour.

A customer writes to an airline about bad service and poor-quality food on a fifteen-hour international flight. The airline, in return, sends a generic e-mail stating that it is sorry and offering the guest five thousand frequent flier miles for his trouble.

Just a generic e-mail? It is not as if there were cafeterias and restaurants the customer could have accessed over the fifteen hours to plan for alternate food arrangements. The least the airline could have done was schedule a call with the customer to listen about the specifics of the problem. After that, maybe they could have sent a fruit-and-cheese basket to say sorry and offered the miles.

A customer calls a television channel, expressing that he has been offended by a recent TV program. The channel sends a personal letter back to the customer, stating, "The channel communicates that the content is developed by production houses, and the channel only aligns with programs that meet its guidelines and values. If the customer wants, he is welcome to address his concerns directly in the next open board meeting."

This is a tough situation, as the television channel is perceived to be in charge of content, but it is not. As the television channel is somewhat helpless in the situation, it is important to include the customer in the solution and give him an opportunity to push the issue further.

In each of the above cases, one gets to know the real character of the other person when both are in a tough situation. Many times, brands put systems in place whereby different customer complaints get various levels of compensation. However, customers do not complain just to get something free. When a customer takes the time to reach out, the compensation offer might make the customer feel uncomfortable. In a way, the immediate offer of five dollars off or five thousand frequent flier miles does two things.

1. The immediate offer of five dollars off or five thousand frequent flier miles implies that the magnitude of duress the customer went through is worth five dollars or five thousand frequent flier miles. If the meal cost sixty dollars or the international flight is valued at seventy-five thousand miles, the offers from the brand might undermine the magnitude of difficulty the brand's errors caused.
2. The customer might feel uncomfortable, as he or she feels the brand thinks he or she called just for the freebies. The brand has made the customer feel that he or she is a freebie digger.

Most customers simply want to share their plight and expect sympathetic listening. That goes a long way in fixing the relationship, as opposed to a direct bribe offer. It is the same way in a relationship when your significant other returns home from work after a tough day; all she wants is for you to listen to her. In that instance, having you as a caring, empathetic listener is critical. The equivalent of the immediate offer of five dollars off or five thousand frequent flier miles would be you giving her a brief hug and saying, "Honey, look, I gave you a hug. Now, grow up, as that is not that big a deal. Let us move on with our evening plans." Sorry, buddy, it is not for you to decide whether it is a big deal or not. The fact that she is sharing it with you tells you that it is a big deal, and you need to adjust your response accordingly.

Brands must realize that their employees are humans. There are times when a guest might not receive the perfect experience, but that is often not the end of the experience. The employee must wait for the opportunity to make amends and show the customer that the brand cares even when it makes a mistake. Most amends should start with the employee listening to the customer without interruption and without feeling any urgency to offer coupons or discounts for the next visit. A future visit cannot be bought. It has to be earned by investing in the relationship with the customer.

The Journey to Better Karma

As I started this book with a promise of good karma, you might have immediately guessed that good karma can only get better over time. The search for better karma inspires a person, as the individual feels excited by the fact that he or she is pushing the envelope to get to something bigger and better. That in itself creates an energy that is ready to change the relationship. When a customer realizes that a brand has gone above and beyond for him or her, that pushes the relationship to the next level and takes a brand closer to a fairy-tale state of ever after. Here are road map elements for the journey to better karma.

- **Getting to Ever After:** A brand must have a clear vision of ever after. The endgame is essential. This inspires a brand to dream big.
- **Celebrating Your Top Customer:** Knowing who your top customer is and celebrating the customer creates an opportunity for the entire brand team to align and be customer focused.

- **Daring to Be Different:** A brand that is truly authentic is comfortable being different and stands for who they are.
- **Seeking Inspiration:** Inspiration is essential for a brand to take the big step forward.
- **Disrupting to Win Big:** Disruption is taking big steps to define your category and industry. This puts your brand in a postition to be the category leader.

Getting to Ever After

My grandma was an excellent cook. She used the simplest of ingredients and made the most incredible, bowl-licking recipes, all served with warmth and a smile. But my grandma's cooking was not bowl-licking-good every day; there were days when she was not in the best of moods. Over time, it became apparent to me that my grandma cooked best when she was happy. If I could make her happy, I was guaranteed bowl-licking-good food.

Over the years, when I heard companies repeat the phrase "Happy team members make happy customers," it reminded me of my observations about my grandmother's cooking. The statement above is tough to dispute, but what is the secret to making it work every time? Recently, I bumped into one answer while shopping at a national department store, where I was astounded by the outstanding level of attentive and relevant customer service I received. This level of service has been so consistent from the store over the years that it is something I have started to expect from the retailer.

So how do they do it? The brand's success is hidden in the brand's motto: "Be everywhere, do everything, and never fail to astonish the customer." Simply stated, it inspires employees to go all the way. I searched the web and found a few more guest-oriented business mottos from other brands, including "We live to serve," "Servin' and lovin' it," "Good people, best service," and "Customer is number one." All the mottos are customer-centric, but the uniqueness of the retail brand's motto is that it tells team members the what, when, and where of customer service standards; the how is left to the team member's discretion. It also clarifies that there is no fine print regarding the customer service; it is everywhere, everything, and never failing. Now that, to me, is a promise of ever after, something one can use as a relationship vow. "I will be there for you everywhere, do everything, and never fail to put a smile on your face" sounds like a relationship promise straight from the heart.

There are numerous theories on achieving the highest level of customer service. I feel the simplest way to achieve is first to hire the right people; tell them what, when, and where to perform; and then leave the how to them. When a brand uses this approach, it can sit back and watch the magic happen, as inspired team members will genuinely wow customers to a new level of service.

Eavesdropping in a Restaurant

Recently, I was sitting at a high-end restaurant, having breakfast, when, at the next table over, a travel-weary couple sat down with their nine-year-old daughter. She was hungry and wanted real food instead of pancakes or waffles. When the family talked to the server, the server informed them that it was still breakfast time and that the lunch items the young girl ordered could not be served for forty-five minutes. The customers protested, the server held his ground, and finally, the server broke the stalemate when he told the customers that he would tell the manager.

I sat in shock at the table next to them. "Let me bring the manager" can never be the final frontier of service. Instead, if the team member had been given the retail brand's motto of customer service, he would have never failed to astonish the customer. The food would have arrived, and there would have been one euphoric nine-year-old, two happy parents, and a few guests at tables surrounding the family all ready to jump up and erupt into a chorus of "Bravo!" and "Encore!" for the customer-friendly experience.

This example brings to the forefront one major issue in serving customers. I call it the safety valve. A safety valve is a statement or action that makes the customer feel that he or she cannot do anything further to make progress in solving an issue. Here are a few examples of commonly used safety valves:

- Let me call the manager.
- Here is a five-dollar gift card for the inconvenience caused.
- I just work here.

If a customer has a serious problem and is discussing that with the employee, anytime the employee utters one of the three sentences above, the discussion is over. The customer has to move on. Now think of a world in which these safety valves do not exist. If a manager clearly explains to his or her employees that each employee is responsible for solving all customer challenges on his or her own and can at no time give a gift card as a response to a customer complaint, then each employee will feel empowered to come to a real solution that will touch the customer. Of course, it might take more time to resolve each customer problem, but the reward for this will be a stronger connection with customers, resulting in long-term relationships.

Celebrating Your Top Customer

Getting to ever after involves an investment, but the investment pays off in a big way. This section illustrates that concept. As I started truly getting it, I realized that team members come first, and the customers come next. I know it is politically correct to say, "Customers come first," but if that is true, then are we not taking for granted the team members who put in long hours to serve those customers? Since I figured this out, I have tried a series of experiments in which I attempted to empower the team members to feel what it takes to put their hearts into a customer experience and truly appreciate a customer. Some of the experiments fell flat on their faces, primarily because they were either too complicated or too engineered.

Celebration Worthy of the Number-One Customer

There was one experiment that truly got the team energized. Anytime I would visit a restaurant in my chain, I would ask the manager and the team to identify their number-one customer for me.

Some managers knew the names of their top customers. The rest could easily run a query and get the names. However, knowing or finding out was not what I was after. First, I would do the math to quantify the monetary value of a customer. Let me say that customer Doe's family bought pizzas from the restaurant once a week and spent on an average thirty-five dollars every time.

That means if you do the math and complete the table below, the numbers are astounding.

How much do you spend per visit?	How many times do you visit in a week?	How much do you spend a year?	How much do you spend in five years?	How much do you spend in ten years?
$35	1	$1,820	$9,100	$18,200

This math usually baffled both managers and team members, and in most cases, the reaction was either "Wow!" or "Can that be true?" When they finally accepted the numbers, all of them agreed that it was an obscene amount of money to spend at a restaurant. As they were stuck in the enlightened moment, I would ask, "When a customer spends that kind of money, shouldn't we know everything about the customer? When is his or her birthday? What does he or she like to do? And once we figure that out, what could we do to show our appreciation for that customer?"

In most cases, restaurant-level team members felt that they were not allowed or empowered to celebrate one customer at a time. They all were given a loyalty program that they were told took care of customers. The restaurant team member's role was simply to make and serve pizzas every day every time.

In this enlightened phase, my goal was making the team at the restaurant feel empowered and showing them how to put their hearts into the initiative. I would then ask each team member to write down one thing we wanted to do to make this customer feel appreciated.

As the team members offered their ideas, I put them into a bowl and then asked the senior-most and the junior-most team members to each pick an idea from the bowl. By now, there was total buy-in of the process, as everyone's ideas had a fair chance of being selected. This is an excellent example of the application of random sampling in the business world to generate buy-in and create enthusiasm.

Now that we had our two top ideas, it was time to act—before the newfound excitement among the team evaporated and each team member returned to his or her prespecified job. On a typical occasion, we would call customers and say that we had a delivery for them. The customers would be baffled and say that they had not ordered anything that day, and we would reply, "We know; it's free."

I would then go to each customer's home, accompanied by ten to twelve team members; the group showed up at the customer's door in uniform. When the family opened the door, they were surprised by balloons, cake, and a high-energy song of appreciation. All this innocent fun happened in the front yard of the customer and lasted three to four minutes. Of course, the unexpected, straight-from-our-hearts gesture always touched the customer, who would inevitably say, "You guys are crazy." The smile on the customer's face told me that it was good crazy.

At the end of the singing, cake, and balloons, the store manager would say to the customer, "We would love to celebrate your patronage by calling next Monday Doe Family Day at our restaurant. We invite you to come make pizzas with us. And for the two hours you work, we would like to donate one hundred dollars to your favorite charity." That was an offer most customers could not say no to, and if the specific day we'd picked did not work, we found another day that worked for the customer.

Now, on Doe Family Day, the restaurant would be fully prepared. The restaurant would have an apron with the name of the customer embroidered on it. The moment the customer came in, he or she would be given the apron and a cap. Then the manager would give the customer a tour of the restaurant. At every point, the team members in the store would recognize the customer and thank him or her for being there that day. After the tour, the customer would work in different places and make a pizza. The customer would be excited when his or her self-made pizza came out of the oven.

Once these customers felt that they were part of the team in the restaurant, what did they do next? The customers would start calling their friends in the neighborhood, and soon their friends would arrive at the store to see this spectacle. When their friends arrived, the customers would give them a tour of the store and introduce them to the team members. By now, each customer usually started referring to the restaurant as "my restaurant." At the end of the day, the manager would take a picture of the customer with the team members and give a copy to the customer.

Now let me take a step back, remove all the excitement and emotions, and objectively evaluate what just happened. First, let me calculate the costs incurred. The costs were as follows:

1. $100 in donation to charity,
2. $50 for uniforms, and
3. $400 in additional labor.

But what did the restaurant gain in return?

1. The team members got a chance to realize that the real value of a customer is not what he or she pays for a given trip or visit. The real value of a customer, if retained over a period, is huge.
2. The team members got a chance to feel the power they had in making a customer happy. As each team member's suggestion had equal weight in selecting how the customer would be celebrated, this exercise made everyone realize that there were no unimportant roles in the store.
3. The act of celebrating customers and then inviting them to the restaurant was a direct way of putting the faces of the customers as a service vision for every store-level employee. No longer were employees making pizzas for unknown customers; they realized that each customer was a human being. If the team members fulfilled or even exceeded someone's needs, that person could become another major spending customer for the restaurant.
4. The customer shifted from thinking of the restaurant as his or her preferred choice of restaurant and started referring to it as "my restaurant."
5. Finally, the service mind-set changed to nurturing a relationship rather than buying the customers' visits.

All of this resulted from a $550 investment. It is tough to quantify the gains made because of $550, but it was clear that the returns were much more than the investment made. The change in the team members' mind-sets would last forever and went a long way in changing the culture of the operations team.

So what will be your next step in going for good customer karma? When will you take the step? If I were in your shoes, the three things I would do based on this information are the following.

1. Identify the value of each customer segment.
2. Identify the opportunity and rewards for moving customers up to the next group.
3. Use the above two pieces of information to determine who your top customers are and how much they spend with you.

Here is something interesting: once you go through these steps and see the dollar value of customers, that information will make action at all levels of your brand inevitable. As you think about this, let me share with you again my grandma's advice: "If you do good karma to others, you will be rewarded with good karma coming back to you." Doing good karma is fun, and it is contagious and rewarding. I can assure you that my grandma was never wrong.

Daring to Be Different

Doing the same thing the same way as everyone else does not result in breakthrough karma. Hence, one has to dare to be different.

If you search online, you will find hundreds of articles on the dos and don'ts of a relationship. In fact, if you search, you will find the best practices for nearly every aspect of life. I believe that being aware of best practices is important in order to open your mind to what others are doing. Then it is time to be you and be bold and daring to be different from everyone else. In the dating experience, you could fall into the predictable category by always showing up to a date with a safe game plan. Your plans for dates might be safe choices one cannot ever go wrong with. You search online for the restaurant that is the number-one recommendation for dates. Next, you make a reservation for an ocean-view table recommended on the site. Now that you have gone with the best recommended plan, you show up with a single rose and a greeting card, sit at the ocean-view table, and await the arrival of your date. All of a sudden, you realize there is a problem. At the next table is another man sitting with a rose. Soon you realize that men with single roses occupy all of the ocean-view tables, waiting for their dates too. You don't feel special anymore. You realize that others too could have searched for the best date restaurant and used the same recommendation. What could you have done differently? You could have taken the dating recommendations as input and then chosen a restaurant that provided a similar ambiance and offered food that your date loves. Instead of a single rose, you could have shown up with a handmade card. In doing so, you would have taken the wisdom of the dating recommendations and made it perfect for you; you would have added a flavor of yourself to the date planning.

A Real Estate Agent Stepping It Up

Recently, I was talking to a good friend of mine who is a Realtor. As I was talking to him, I learned that Realtors have operated a big part of real estate the same way for years. For a buyer, any agent will print a list of homes based on the same multiple listing service (MLS) listing. For a seller, any real estate agent will do a real estate price comparison report that lists the sale prices of similar homes in the area. Both these reports are in real estate language and not user friendly. They have every piece of information available on the homes. As I was learning, I pushed my friend to be different in a customer-centric way. Here were a few thoughts.

- Consider adding the following to your report for a seller:
    - index the comparative homes based on the actual sales prices;
    - for the homes that indexed high on the sales price, identify the variables that separated them from the rest;
    - do a seasonality report to show when houses sell fast and when houses sell slowly in the neighborhood; and
    - showcase the relationship of a number of days in the market versus approximately how much money the seller loses every month by holding the house.

If my real estate friend can put all this information in a custom report for the seller, he will bring significant value-added insights to the seller. This will be different from the traditional price comparison reports.

- Consider adding the following to the report for the buyer:
    - a neighborhood map with all the school bus stops marked so that a family can immediately visualize how far the kids will have to walk to go to school and
    - research and a story of the neighborhood.

The neighborhood story could include facts like the following:

- The community is active, and every year, members have a Christmas light competition.
- The community has socials and barbecues at the swimming pool during summer.
- Safety is important for the community, and every year, local police officers visit the clubhouse to educate residents and answer any questions.
- Based on information from the local home improvement store, the flowers that are perfect for the local soil are hybrid roses and lilies.

- Synthesize the MLS listing by making a spreadsheet that only has the key attributes the buyer's family is looking for. Every time you take them out, fill the first row of the spreadsheet with the listings you plan to show them that day. The seller will have this simple custom form prepared for them and can take notes in it after each home visit. That way, the discussion at the end of the day is more meaningful.

As I started rattling off all these ideas, initially, there was some hesitation and resistance from my friend. He was stuck in the logic that safety comes from doing the same things the same way. However, it did not take him long to realize that selling homes by going outside the box would be fun. He added to the brainstorming, as he could see the excitement in the eyes of his customers once he rolled out his new customer-assistance strategy.

The Magic of a Pizza Cheese Pull

During the pizza-marketing phase of my career, I realized that pizza on television advertising is usually marked by a cheese pull. A cheese pull is when the eater bites into the pizza and gently pulls the pizza away, creating the visual of a magical cheese pull. History has shown that a cheese pull creates instant food cravings that push the viewer to order pizza at that instant. The goal of the cheese pull is to make your mouth water; the advertiser wants to focus the viewer's attention on the gooey goodness of ng strings of cheese and create an appetite appeal. As I was getting ready to plan the storyboard for the advertising, I asked myself, "Are all cheese pulls the same? Why can't I find the cheese pull that is better than any other traditional cheese pulls?"

Asking the question itself was important, as now I had created a curiosity in my mind that I could not ignore. Within a few weeks, I designed a customer research approach that would study different people doing the cheese pull. I broke up the cheese-pull models by age, gender, body type, and other factors. For men, I added categories for different types of facial hair too. Once I had an exhaustive list of cheese-pull models, I embarked on a photo shoot to create cheese-pull pictures for each model. Finally, I was ready for the customer test. As I was getting ready for the results of the customer test, I was getting worried. What if the research showed that all cheese pulls were the same? If that happened, then I was in big trouble for spending an obscene amount of money for nothing. I feared I might lose my job over this cheese-pull obsession. However, it was too late to do anything about it.

When the results came in, the first thing I learned was that all cheese pulls are not created equal. The learning and insights from the study were broader than simply who pulls off the best cheese pull on television. Here are some of the key things I learned.

- There was a significant drop in appeal when the same person took a bite of pizza without doing a cheese pull, validating the power of the cheese pull. The appeal was even lower for a person posing for a picture and pretending to eat. When probed, respondents said, "Why is he not eating the pizza? Is he going to actually eat it? Is there something wrong with the pizza that he doesn't want to bite down?"
- The appeal was low for an attractive young woman doing a cheese pull. The reason can be summarized by one respondent's comment: "I had to go back to the picture to see the pizza, as I had missed it completely the first time."

- Kids doing a cheese pull also had a low appeal, as that made the respondents believe this was kids' pizza and relevant to an occasion for a kid's party. They also expected the price of this pizza to be low. This was not a pizza parents were excited to eat themselves.
- Just to have fun, I put in some pictures of celebrities doing cheese pulls. When people saw these images, they thought the pictures were some kind of PR or news story.
- One of the highest appeals was for a slightly overweight African American man with big eyes and no facial hair doing the cheese pull. As I studied this more, I realized no facial hair was essential for a successful cheese pull. The big eyes drew attention to the cheese pull and demonstrated the excitement. The ideal skin tone was one that was the right background and brought out the contrast in the cheese pull.

If you are wondering, the ads with better cheese pulls did drive higher sales. The underlying lesson in my experience in pizza marketing is about paying attention to the details and not being scared to challenge existing ways of thinking. Beyond cheese pulls, this journey created a huge buzz in the team and opened the mind of everyone to going beyond traditional thinking. As with cheese pulls, every brand has established ways of marketing. In contrast, I do not know how successful the real estate strategy will be, but I know my good friend has started the journey to separate himself from the rest. He might make a few mistakes, but I believe making new mistakes is a guaranteed way to get to new levels of success.

This quote[7] from Michael Jordan about how failures drove him to succeed is my favorite. I have the poster in my office, and every time I fail, I read the quote and get excited about new possibilities: "I've missed more than nine thousand shots in my career. I've lost almost three hundred games. Twenty-six times, I've been trusted to take the game-winning shot and missed. I've failed over and over and over again in my life. And that is why I succeed."

I believe it is important to challenge the existing thinking in all aspects of life and find out ways to make processes significantly better. In a category where doing the same has become the norm, a change will get noticed and make an impact. This way, you are not going to be sitting at a restaurant at an ocean-view table with a rose, surrounded by other dates doing the same.

Seeking Inspiration

As a brand thinks of ways to differentiate its offering, it needs to be open to inspiration. Inspiration can come from places you are least likely to expect.

Grandma's Story about King Bruce

My grandma used to tell me the story of Robert the Bruce, king of Scotland, who spent his life in battles with the king of England. Six times, he lost. After the loss in the sixth battle, he was hiding in a cave with a few of his closest generals. They were all wounded, and King Bruce was ready to give up. As he sat in the cave, he saw a spider trying to weave a web from one side of the cave to the other. The spider tried to throw its web thread from one side of the cave to the other but did not make it. It fell to the ground, picked itself up, and went back up. It tried again and failed. This happened six times, and now King Bruce and his generals were eagerly watching what the spider would do next. The spider gently walked up the cave wall and jumped. This time, it landed on the other side, and soon it started weaving a large web. Watching the spider succeed, King Bruce jumped up and said that he was ready to try for the seventh time. In the seventh battle, he beat the king of England. Every time my grandma told me the story, I used to stare at her face and observe her excitement as the spider made it on the seventh try. I never tried to find out the complete story of King Bruce, as this version I heard from my grandma has been special to me.

Over the years, I realized that there was a second piece of wisdom in the story, regarding where one can get inspiration from. In the case of King Bruce, it came from a spider in a cave. Hence, one has to keep his or her eyes and ears open, as inspiration can come from anywhere.

I have tried to apply this concept in the business world, as I have learned that by looking outside the industry, one can get a broader perspective and a bigger inspiration.

Visiting a Casino and Getting a Massage

When a retail chain asked me to assist them in building a loyalty program, I decided to pause and seek inspiration outside the retail industry. I started studying how casinos take care of their guests, how a national massage chain handles an ongoing reward program, how an airline rewards different customers based on the miles they fly, and how an upscale restaurant chain approaches customer service. As I sat back and reflected on each of the programs, I realized I could build a loyalty program that was truly next generation. Without this insight, I would have simply built a loyalty program marginally better than that of the biggest competitor to my retail client.

In the relationship world, inspiration is also important. Otherwise, one starts to repeat the same ideas in different ways, and the relationship gets boring. Instead of a dozen roses, a gift becomes two dozen roses or a mixed flower bouquet, with a card every time. One time, I was sitting with a good friend of mine before Christmas, and he was complaining that it was tough to buy a gift for his wife every year. He could not get outside his list of a sweater, jewelry, flowers, and chocolates. He was sharing with me the story of his engagement to her, when he did not have money to buy a ring. He made a cool ring out of a gum wrapper and used it to propose to her. He still remembered the sparkle in her eyes that day. He had never been able to recreate that. As we sat and talked, I realized that my friend was ready for a breakthrough idea, and the only thing missing was some out-of-the-box inspiration. I went online and started reading to him strange gift ideas, and all of a sudden, he stood up in excitement just like King Bruce and said, "I've got it! The best things my wife has given me are my four kids and, of course, every day of our life together. I will get her a charm bracelet that will have a charm for each of my four kids. And then, during the year, for different special occasions, I will get her charms to celebrate moments in our life together." I stared at my friend in admiration, as he had broken away from the routine gift list. I was proud of him, and I was sure that when he gave the charm bracelet to his wife, she would have the same sparkle in her eye that she'd had on the day of his proposal.

In both the business and the relationship world, one needs three things to get to a breakthrough idea:

1. a desire to go beyond ordinary,
2. determination to not get disheartened by failures, and
3. openness to inspiration, which can come from anywhere.

Let us work on an example together. A retail brand wants to create a reward program for its customers. In most cases, the brand will start by identifying what its key competition is doing and then engage a smart vendor to recommend a next step. The vendor comes up with an idea to send a five-dollar gift card to its loyal customers after they spend $100.

Before we go that route, let us pause and seek some inspiration. Let us ask a few of the brand's team members to examine reward programs in each of the following areas.

1. Airlines: Airlines have found great ways to reward their loyal customers. An upgrade to first class is a value that really sinks in with a loyal customer.

2. A National Massage Chain: The company has found a way to offer loyal customers a steep discount that only the loyal customers get. That creates a great value perception.

3. Casinos: Like the airlines, they too go out of their way to make loyal customers feel special by upgrading their hotel rooms to suites and offering free food and beverages during their stays.

We can go on with examples of inspiration. But if we stay with only these three and reflect on them, we might realize that the idea of sending a five-dollar gift card to loyal customers after they spend a hundred dollars does not have the same impact as the approaches of the three industries we looked at. The inspiration from these other industries will push the brand to go beyond. Why not offer the loyal customers something others cannot get? Why not offer them

1. a separate expedited checkout line,
2. a separate no-wait return line,
3. preferred parking during the holiday season, or
4. a beverage-and-snack area where they can take refreshment breaks during a visit?

More inspiration means even bigger ideas, and it is exciting to see that a few sources of inspiration can make a brand start thinking outside the box and come up with big ways of celebrating customers. These big investments in customer karma are bound to have big returns.

Disruption to Win Big

The world is changing, and it is changing faster today than it did yesterday. My grandma was excited to have a landline phone in her home, and she used the same phone all her life. She was ingenious in connecting a long wire to the phone so that she could take the phone to any room in the house. Today, if I have the same cell phone for two years, my friends keep reminding me that it is time to upgrade to a newer one. As waves of rapid change continuously hit our world, newer ideas evolve, constantly disrupting the current way of doing business. In the business world of today, even though most brands are focusing on innovation, disruption to the category and a new way of fulfilling customer needs come from brands outside. Look at resource-sharing brands, such as Uber and Airbnb. As they showcase how surplus assets can be monetized, traditional brands in the spaces must realize that the days of traditional competition are over. A threat can come from anywhere, not just direct competition. In the same way, opportunities can come from unexpected areas. Think about how car-buying patterns will change with Uber becoming more popular. Won't bigger sedans with comfortable backseats be more in demand? In the case of Airbnb and similar sites becoming more and more popular, how can future home designs change? I expect houses to have more suites with external entrances and their own bathrooms and minikitchens. This way, the future resource will be designed for perfect sharing. Impact on design is simply one dimension of the changes coming in the future.

As I worked with brands from different industries, I found that most brands wanted to take bold steps to be better. This desire to be better comes from a balance of being cautious and making efforts to continue to improve. There is always an eye to incremental costs and marginal return on investment. Somehow, brands feel compelled to make sure that the incremental investment in customers is worth it. The equivalent of this in a relationship would be, for example, a man asking, "Why do I need to be nicer to my significant other unless the action will make her jump up and down in excitement?" I feel there are times when a brand needs to completely break things down and do an overhaul by starting afresh. That, to me, is the only way a brand can take a giant next step and separate itself from its competition.

However, all changes don't have to be that big. There are simple changes brands can implement that will result in big gains in customer karma. Let me indulge and share a few simple stories that showcase directions brands today can take to redefine customer experience. In each case, the brand manager's eyes lit up after hearing the idea, but then he or she dismissed the idea by claiming it was too out there or too risky or by saying, "We can be successful without taking steps this bold." I understand that brand managers have to be accountable for the risks they take, but I believe these are ideas that will separate brands. So I want to ask you, will you visit these brands?

A Restaurant That Closes at Lunch When It Is Full

Most quick-service restaurants maximize their business during lunch. As a brand pushes for new sales, more customers come to it during lunch. If a brand is designed to serve a maximum of 100 customers per hour, what happens when 120 customers show up? There is a possibility that operations might not be able to offer the same level of service to all 120 customers. Maybe the rush of incremental customers forces the brand to offer an 80 percent service level to all customers. This might not be helpful in creating repeat visits among this group, as the brand's perception and experience-delivery system get diluted as customers start getting lower levels of service.

Now, if the brand is serious about service and decides to turn on a We Are Full Now sign when it is at capacity during lunch, how will you feel? Will you be upset and offended and never return? Or will you appreciate the restaurant's commitment and plan ahead more the next time you visit the restaurant? As a customer, I will respect the restaurant brand for being serious about its level of customer service. In the future, I might try to make a reservation to make sure I get a seat.

A Checkout Lounge in Your Neighborhood Supermarket

Every time you are at a supermarket and have a cartful of groceries, you stand in line behind another customer with roughly the same number of purchases. On the other side, there are special lines for those buying fewer than twenty items and even-more-expedited lines for those who are buying fewer than ten items. As you stand in the long line, you wish you were buying fewer than twenty items. What would your reaction be if the supermarket created a small lounge area at the checkout for those making a large amount of purchases? When you get to the checkout area, an employee takes over your cart. You are taken to a lounge area where you relax in a massage chair and have a bottle of ice water or a latte to enjoy. You sit back, close your eyes for a minute, and simply appreciate this gift. As you are relaxing, the store employee checks out all your purchases and arranges them in your bags. You pay and then choose to relax there for another five minutes before you head to the car.

Will this level of service from your supermarket make you freak out? Or will you simply adopt the supermarket as the only place you ever go to buy things?

A Gas Station That Does Not Have Any Prices Advertised

Are you tired of all the nines in the prices advertised by gas stations? What would be your reaction to a gas station that charges you the average price of all gas stations within five miles? You do not have to worry about paying too much. The average price is computed daily, and that is what the station charges you.

Would you still go anywhere else searching for low prices? With this method, you are assured that you will always be on the side of savings with this gas station.

An Airline That Gives an Extra Hour to Business Customers

As a senior executive, every time you leave for a business trip from your office, you usually have a long line of people who need to talk to you before your trip. Somehow, your impending absence creates an artificial crisis in which these micromeetings are a must. Some airlines offer a limo service to the airport for business travelers. You can easily afford a limo ride to the airport if that is what you want, so what can the airline give you to make you say, "Wow"? Imagine the airline offering you a two-way limo ride that will take you and your team to the airport and then bring your team back to the office after dropping you off at the airport. This way, you get a priceless extra hour with your team. You are also relaxed and worry-free, as you are guaranteed to make the flight, as you have checked in with the airline's limo.

Will this sensitivity make you choose this airline for all your business travels? What is the value of the extra hour to you before your business trip?

An Auto Insurance Company Charges You for the Miles You Drive

Do you understand the logic behind auto insurance charges? The only thing you know is that your insurance premium will go up if you get a traffic ticket. What will be your reaction if an auto insurance company wants to simplify the insurance premium? The new insurance company wants to break its premium into two areas: a fixed amount for the fixed cost and a price-per-mile-driven cost for the variable part of the insurance. That means in months when you drive less, you pay less.

Don't you think this is fair? If an auto insurance company implements a plan like this, why would you go anywhere else?

An Auto Repair Company That Is Completely Transparent

Every time you drop your car at an auto repair shop, do you worry about what the shop will do to your car? Do you worry they will replace parts that do not actually need to be replaced? What will be your reaction if the auto repair shop gives you access to a website that is a live web feed of your car's repair? Anytime the technician needs to show you something, he texts you, and you can see in the live video what he is referring to. Also, you do not have to wonder when your car will be ready, as you can see the progress being made. If an auto repair shop offered this kind of access to your repair, would you go anywhere else?

Now take a moment to think of the answers to these five questions.

1. Will the restaurant that closes for lunch when it is full become your favorite restaurant?
2. Will the supermarket that has a checkout lounge for customers spending a lot become the only supermarket you like to visit?
3. Will the airline that offers a two-way limo be your first choice for business travels?
4. Will the gas station with no price advertised be the only gas station that you visit?
5. Will the auto repair shop with a live feed of your repair be the only place you take your car for repair?

Even if you do not immediately switch to these brands, if you are seriously considering these brands, it shows that good customer karma results in good karma for the brand. In each case, the brand did not worry about the cost of the service it offered you, nor did it worry about who did what. In all cases, the brand simply put your needs first and wanted to make the experience better for you. As a result, the brands will be rewarded with a lifetime relationship with their customers, as they do good customer karma with their customer-centered thinking.

Final Words

The customer-karma journey starts with the first visit by a customer, which is equivalent to a first date. The goal of the journey is to build a long-term relationship with the customer, which is equivalent to a marriage. But once the long-term relationship status is attained, is the journey over? What happens next?

I believe that once a brand attains a long-term relationship with its customers, it should first pause and celebrate with pride this incredible accomplishment achieved through internal alignment and a strong focus on what the customer wants. However, building a long-term relationship is just the beginning, just as a couple will face new challenges after they get through the first five years of marriage. The journey forward will be similar to what brought the brand this far, but with stronger commitment, as the customer now blindly trusts the brand.

Here are seven areas the brand needs to look at as it continues its journey to extend its relationship with the customer.

Know the Value of Your Customers

If there is one thing you do based on reading this book, please consider identifying the value of each customer segment and then identifying the opportunity for moving customers up to the next loyalty group. The power of this information is that it makes action inevitable. Once your brand realizes how moving one customer a week to the next level impacts your sales, this knowledge will change the culture of your organization.

Avoid (Bad) Surprises

Avoiding bad surprises primarily refers to ensuring the customer has a consistent expectation of service standards and levels that cannot go down. Consistency has three elements:

a. every day (not just today but always over time),
b. every store (not just one store but everywhere), and
c. every team member (not just one person one time but every team member).

In short, the customer says, "You earned my business by validating your commitment to serving me over time. Now that I am using you exclusively, I want you to make sure that the service commitments remain the same or go up." Going back to the dating example, this is similar to a new spouse saying, "You wooed me when we were dating with cards, flowers, and other ways of showing your affection. I chose you because of who you are and all your actions. Now that we are in a marriage, I do not expect those actions to cease. I will be disappointed if you start ignoring me now."

Recognize the Customer and Continue to Make the Customer Feel Special

During the dating phase, the customer was looking at multiple options. But over the period of dating, the customer experienced the superior product offering from the brand and today considers him- or herself its loyal customer. As a loyal customer, he or she expects the brand to recognize him or her. Team members should know his or her name, and the customer should get special treatment for being in the elite group of loyal customers. A good example would be what an airline offers on a flight: while other passengers wait, only the loyal customers board the aircraft first. In short, customers want the dream promised in the television series *Cheers*:[8] a place "where everybody knows your name."

Prove to the Customer That Trusting You Was Justified

Trust is an important factor today, especially as loyal customers share a lot of their personal information and behavior patterns with brands they follow. Customers want the brand to treat all information cautiously and never break the trust. A break in trust not only breaks the relationship but also makes the customer feel stupid for trusting the brand. The trust also involves product content, facts shared about the company, and all other details. Sharing with integrity is important for businesses, just as it is important in a relationship. Without integrity, one can be easily perceived as deceptive.

Be a Good Citizen

Being a good citizen has become an extension of a customer's expectation. In the ever-changing world, customers expect brands to first be good neighbors and give back to the community and world at large. Customers expect brands to be aware of the world they are in and make sincere efforts to make things better. Focus on sustainability is important, as that shows a commitment to leaving the world in a better state. Being there for the community in times of need and investing in the increased well-being of the community are part of being a good citizen. It creates a good feeling when the brand creates good karma.

Never Forget That You and the Customer Are in a Relationship

This is simple. Once a customer becomes a loyal customer, often, he or she chooses to endorse the brand on social media or with friends. That means the customer is comfortable being seen in public in association with the brand. If the brand does something that the customer considers to be misbehaving, then the customer might feel embarrassed by the brand. Some examples of misbehavior include advertisements considered improper by the mainstream media, endorsement of divisive social or political causes by a brand founder or spokesperson, or violations of the law. Simply stated, earlier, the brand was enjoying a single life; now it is in a relationship. Being in a relationship means you must act with responsibility, as your actions impact others who are close to you.

Be Authentic

Finally, it is essential to be authentic. That is the only way to be. Initially, the title of this book was *Marperations*, as I intended to focus on how marketing, operations, and different departments should work together for one goal. After I finished the book, I saw the following challenges.

- What is the common goal that everyone in a company should try to get to together as a team? Without defining that goal, it is tough to align everyone. I also realized that goal should be something that everyone wants to achieve, a promise so enchanting that it will draw everyone in. That realization gave rise to the importance of customer karma, a journey that humanizes the customer experience and inspires the entire company to strive toward a lifetime relationship with customers.
- A book on marperations sounded like a book on corporate reorganization, in which departments are realigned to become more efficient. I have gone through numerous reorganizations, and most times, the reorganization was about a reduction in jobs. I did not enjoy doing that, and hence, I felt more connected as the advocate of customer karma instead of marperations.
- More than anything else, I could not see myself holding a book called *Marperations*. It was not me. Even though the book was ready, I chose to completely rewrite it, as I realized there is no shortcut to authenticity.

As you can see, the journey never stops; it is ongoing and is marked by constant improvement. Just like in a marriage, in a relationship with customers, a brand needs to grow over time and stay current with the needs of the customer. Being current with the customer's needs and putting ongoing effort toward doing good karma for the customer will be rewarded in the long term.

I want to finish by reminding you of my late grandma's words: "Do good karma in life. If you do good karma to others, you will be rewarded with good karma coming back to you." My grandma was never wrong.

Endnotes

1. Clay Dover, "CMO Perspectives: Arjun Sen of ZenMango," *Nation's Restaurant News*, April 14, 2015, http://nrn.com/advertising/cmo-perspectives-arjun-sen-zenmango.

2. *Wikipedia*, s.v. "AIDA," last modified March 10, 2016, https://en.wikipedia.org/wiki/AIDA_(marketing).

3. *Oxford Dictionaries*, s.v. "loyalty," accessed April 14, 2016, http://www.oxforddictionaries.com/us/definition/american_english/loyalty.

4. Gary Marshall, *Pretty Woman* (Beverly Hills, CA: Touchstone Pictures, 1990), DVD.

5. Manna Dey, vocal performance of "Jodi Kagoje Lekho Naam," on *Legends*, produced by Sa Re Ga Ma.

6. Ron Underwood, *City Slickers* (Abiquiú, NM: Metro-Goldwyn-Mayer Studios Inc., 1991), DVD.

7. Michael Jordan, "Failure," Nike commercial, 2006.

8. James Burrows, *Cheers* (Boston, MA: Charles/Burrows/Charles Productions, Paramount Television, 1982), DVD.

Open Book Editions
A Berrett-Koehler Partner

Open Book Editions is a joint venture between Berrett-Koehler Publishers and Author Solutions, the market leader in self-publishing. There are many more aspiring authors who share Berrett-Koehler's mission than we can sustainably publish. To serve these authors, Open Book Editions offers a comprehensive self-publishing opportunity.

A Shared Mission

Open Book Editions welcomes authors who share the Berrett-Koehler mission—Creating a World That Works for All. We believe that to truly create a better world, action is needed at all levels—individual, organizational, and societal. At the individual level, our publications help people align their lives with their values and with their aspirations for a better world. At the organizational level, we promote progressive leadership and management practices, socially responsible approaches to business, and humane and effective organizations. At the societal level, we publish content that advances social and economic justice, shared prosperity, sustainability, and new solutions to national and global issues.

Open Book Editions represents a new way to further the BK mission and expand our community. We look forward to helping more authors challenge conventional thinking, introduce new ideas, and foster positive change.

For more information, see the Open Book Editions website: http://www.iuniverse.com/Packages/OpenBookEditions.aspx

Join the BK Community! See exclusive author videos, join discussion groups, find out about upcoming events, read author blogs, and much more! http://bkcommunity.com/

CPSIA information can be obtained at www.ICGtesting.com
Printed in the USA
LVOW11*0325290916

506685LV00002B/3/P

- Marketing = dating (AIDA)
  <u>A</u>wareness, <u>I</u>nterest, <u>D</u>esire, & <u>A</u>ction
- Dating analogy is great
- Golf story, + M Jordan are great
- Never mentions Tiger by name